EMBROIDERY BACKGROUNDS

PAINTING & DYEING TECHNIQUES

EMBROIDERY BACKGROUNDS

PAINTING & DYEING
TECHNIQUES

Pauline Brown

B. T. Batsford Ltd · London

ISBN 0 7134 3660 3

Filmset by Latimer Trend & Company Ltd,
Plymouth
Printed and bound in Great Britain by
Anchor Brendon Ltd, Tiptree, Essex
for the publishers
B. T. Batsford Ltd.
4 Fitzhardinge Street
London W1H 0AH

Frontispiece: *Three evening bags, each
depicting a different method of colouring.
The shell-shaped framed bag in cotton satin
has been sprayed in gold and coral. It is
lightly quilted and embroidered with tiny
glass beads and French knots. The round
bag, tritik gathered and dyed in purple and
pink, is enhanced with silver metal thread
couching and herringbone stitch. In the third
example, batik 'crackle' and plain-dyed off-
cuts are combined with machine-embroidered
silk*

CONTENTS

Acknowledgment   7
Introduction   9

1 **Historical background**   11

2 **Approaches: Methods and
   Experiments**   14
   General hints   17

3 **Tie-dye**   18
   General equipment   18
   Equipment for tying   20
   Equipment for clamping   21
   Fabrics   21
   Dyes   21
   Methods   25
   Experiments   43

4 **Batik**   57
   Equipment for waxing   57
   Equipment for dyeing   61
   Fabrics   61
   Dyes   63
   General method for batik   63
   Transferring the design   63
   Preparation of fabric   63
   Method   63
   Experiments   67

5 Painting, Spraying and Drawing 81
Painting and spraying 81
Silk paints 92
Transfer paints and crayons 95
Drawing 97
Experiments 98

6 Embroidery Techniques 108
Stitches 108
Quilting 113
Appliqué 116
Beads 119
Patchwork 121
Manipulating fabrics 123

Appendices
 I Fabric categories 126
 II Suitability of fabrics for painting
   and dyeing 127
   Suppliers 129
   Book List 132
   Index 133

ACKNOWLEDGMENT

I should like to thank all those friends and students, including the girls of St Michael's Grammar School, Finchley, who lent me their work to photograph; also my thanks to Martin Gould and Bret Sampson for taking the photographs and to Dee McLean for her line illustrations.

I am grateful to the following firms who sent me fabrics, dyes and paints with which to experiment: Berol Ltd, Binney & Smith (Europe) Ltd, Deka Textilfarben, Dryad, Dylon International Ltd, Geo. Rowney & Co. Ltd, Geo. Weil & Sons Ltd, Whaleys (Bradford) Ltd and Winsor & Newton.

Last but not least, thanks to my family – to my daughter Mandy for reading the text, to my son Martin for his designs and to my husband John for his continuing help and support.

INTRODUCTION

Embroidery today, for both the amateur and the professional, can be one of the most exciting and rewarding crafts. As it can have both practical and decorative uses, the bounds to which traditional techniques can be stretched are almost limitless. In art schools, the subject has been accepted as a fine art and it is possible to obtain a degree in embroidery. Students experiment with and explore techniques and materials to produce works which to an outsider might not at first come under the heading of embroidery – textile art might be a more appropriate description. However, many of these creations, both two and three-dimensional, are based on traditional methods. Colleges of Further Education in the UK run City and Guilds courses to train teachers of embroidery and in schools and adult education classes work of high quality, both in design and technique, is often produced.

In all these categories the emphasis nowadays is on creativity and in recent years there has been a move to combine a number of techniques in one piece of work: canvaswork can be used with appliqué, patchwork and quilting with additional creative stitchery, and three-dimensional projects may use any number of new ideas to achieve the required result.

However, the most recent innovation, particularly among professionals and more advanced students, has been the addition of paint and dyes to embroidery. I first became interested in creating backgrounds of this type for my embroidery when I was studying at the London College of Fashion. I experimented with various methods of colouring fabric, and became so fascinated with the effects that plain cloth seemed to lack any interest at all. The shades and combinations of colours which can be produced are unending, and experimental pieces and even so-called failures can sometimes be reassessed and used to effect.

This book offers you the opportunity to find out ways and means of producing exciting and individual backgrounds for your work, using tie-dye and batik, and with painting and spraying. It also suggests other approaches with dyes and paints which can enhance, highlight or reinforce the design of your embroidery. Of course, experimentation is necessary, but this is part of the fun.

All the colouring methods described can be carried out in your kitchen or workroom with the minimum of trouble and most with equipment and utensils which are readily available. As for the embroidery, quilting, surface, stitchery, appliqué, beads and machine embroidery can all combine with paints and dyes to produce new and creative work.

1 HISTORICAL BACKGROUND

The decoration of fabric by embroidery, painting and dyeing began in the mists of antiquity. It is probable that of these three skills embroidery came first, when simple needles were invented to seam animal skins together and subsequently to add some primitive form of decoration. The first painting of fabric using colouring from the earth, plants and berries would probably have been contemporary with the cave paintings of prehistory.

The ancient Egyptians used painted images on coarse linen votive cloths in about 1500 BC. These depicted such scenes as man making an appropriate offering to a god. Linen mummy cloths of the first century BC have also been found with painted decoration showing the Egyptian gods, and cotton cloths from later tombs have inscriptions in pen and gilt.

The origins of resist methods of dyeing – tie-dye and batik – also go back many thousands of years and possibly developed simultaneously in places as far apart as Asia and South America. Early examples of tie-dye come from both Tibet, from where there are very primitive examples of tie-dyed felt, and Peru, where an alpaca cloth of the first or second century BC tie-dyed in yellow, green and brown, has been discovered. In the East, tie-dye is generally believed to have started in

Central Asia and spread through India and across to Africa. At the same time, it gradually found its way along the old silk routes to China and Japan. There is an Indian folk legend which tells of a love-lorn prince, who, when he wrote a letter to his princess in a far distant land, bound it tightly with coloured cords. During its long journey, the letter became soaked by the monsoon rains and the coloured cords and the parchment shed their dye. The princess was so delighted with her beautifully patterned letter that she agreed to marry the prince at once. Thus tie-dye is said to have been born. Similarly, batik probably originated in Asia, and spread through Malaysia to South-East Asia, Indonesia, China and Japan. In many third world countries today, beautiful native work in tie-dye and batik is still carried on, employing traditional methods. Natural dyes, such as indigo and cochineal, are sometimes used, but more generally chemical dyes have taken precedence. In Indonesia, Malaysia and Sri Lanka, artists are producing works both pictorial and abstract in form, as well as dress fabrics of traditional design, and in India and West Africa tie-dye fabrics in traditional patterns are still used for garments. The Yoruba tribe of Nigeria and the Senegalese dyers create stitched designs as a resist to the indigo dye. These result in

intricate all-over patterns in white on blue. In addition, the West African dyers use as a resist a paste made of cassava flour which is painted or stencilled on to the cotton cloth before dyeing.

In the majority of cases, these resist methods do not have the addition of embroidery, although there are now machine-embroidered tie-dye shirts and kaftan-type robes, produced in Sierra Leone and Gambia for the tourist market. Indian garments such as wedding saris are sometimes embroidered with gold threads and shisha mirrors giving an exotic effect; quilted jackets in tie-dyed fabrics are regularly exported to appeal to Western taste. However, for combining paints and dyes with embroidery, the Japanese are the undoubted masters. The beautiful kimonos of the seventeenth- and eighteenth-century Edo period display unrivalled and immaculate technique and design. Exquisite stencilled and painted designs abound in combination with gold thread and silk embroidery; figured satins are tie-dyed and embroidered with plum or cherry tree designs; tie-dyed trellis patterns are worked on hemp with gold and red embroidered flowers trailing in profusion; landscapes have pines or bamboo motifs superimposed on painted rivers and seas. Many of these textiles exhibit designs made up of thousands of closely packed tritik dots forming areas of texture or decorative motifs.

In England, which has had a wonderful tradition of embroidery from twelfth-century Opus Anglicanum onwards, there is little early evidence of its use with paints or dyes. A late sixteenth-century example appears on the back of a fragment of embroidery worked by Mary, Queen of Scots. This shows a strap-work design enclosing a stylized bird and flowers painted on satin and including some appliqué. Not until the late eighteenth century did the combination of embroidery and paint become widespread, when there was a vogue for needlework pictures combined with water colour. The original design was drawn, or sometimes printed, on white silk taffeta, with the finer details such as faces and hands, and quite often the sky, delicately painted. The remainder of the picture would then be worked in coloured silk threads in long and short stitch. Chenille threads were also used to give texture to such items as trees and bushes. Subjects ranged from sentimental pastoral scenes of shepherdesses to pictures taken from engravings by famous artists of the day. There is an example in the Victoria and Albert Museum, of about 1800, of 'Fame strewing flowers on Shakespeare's Tomb' from a picture by Angelica Kauffmann, and several others are in the Lady Lever Gallery at Port Sunlight. The Embroiderers' Guild has a fragment of a waistcoat of the same period, which incorporates into the delicate silk floral embroidery a small painted medallion showing a classical figure. This is sewn to the white satin background with a circlet of spangles.

Painting on fabric gradually became a popular pursuit of the nineteenth century. There was a fashion for painting on velvet – one of the accomplishments of a young lady of the 1840s. Very often vegetable dyes were used, or oil paints could be purchased from the local emporium. The Victoria and Albert Museum owns a box, containing paints, which was used specifically for this purpose. The Victorians, who pursued handicrafts avidly, were keen on mixing different techniques, and examples exist of canvaswork pieces, and others worked on a silk or satin ground, where some areas are painted.

In the early twentieth century there are only isolated instances of the use of paint with embroidery – metal threads were occasionally painted to resemble *or nué*, and an individual needlewoman might add some water colour to an embroidered picture. The 1920s and '30s saw a fashion for stencilling and block printing. An article in *Needle Art* of 1922 was devoted to block printing combined with embroidery for useful household items such as bags, table runners and lampshades. The same

magazine a few years later includes transfers for 'deft brush or needle' to be stencilled, painted or embroidered.

Apart from a few experiments by individuals there was little subsequent use of paints and dyes with embroidery until about 1970. The 1960s had seen a set-back in the attraction of tie-dye due, possibly, to its 'hippy' image when used on T-shirts, and this situation was not reversed until the importation of attractive cotton tie-dyed garments from India a decade later, when all types of ethnic-style clothes became popular. As far as embroiderers are concerned, the first sprayed design did not appear until 1971 in an exhibition by the 62 Group of the Embroiderers' Guild, but since then the use of painting and dyeing, and particularly spraying, has been a constituent of many artists' work.

2 APPROACHES: METHODS & EXPERIMENTS

There are several approaches to adopt when considering the use of tie-dye, batik or painting of fabric as additional colour for your embroidery. You must decide whether the use of such methods is to be the most important aspect of the final design, or whether it is to be used either to emphasize or simply to enhance the embroidery which will subsequently be worked. If planning the work as an embroiderer, then most probably it will be the actual stitchery which will tend to be uppermost in your mind, and this aspect of the work will be the one which you will prefer to be of most significance. It is essential that the colour contributes to the project something which could not otherwise be done in embroidery – the colouring method should enhance the finished piece, not detract from it.

If looking at the work from the opposite point of view, that is as a painter would, then it will be the dyeing, batik or application of paint which will probably have most emphasis. In this case the embroidery acts as a reinforcement to the colour, highlighting certain areas or adding texture. If you make the mistake of adding too much embroidery to an intricately patterned fabric in, for example, batik, which can produce quite complex designs, there is a danger of destroying the effect which has previously been created.

When you first begin painting and dyeing fabric, experimentation can lead to exciting and unexpected results, some of which will give you inspiration for subsequent designs. Even if, with your initial efforts, the imagined result does not occur, you will have a ready-made collection of unusual materials in a wide spectrum of colour combinations and patterns. Try the same technique but use different sorts of fabric: tie-dye cotton, silk, linen, wool, towelling or corduroy; batik on any natural fibres; spray or paint on almost anything! Use colours together which you would not normally combine and they will in turn spark off new ideas. You will be surprised at the variety of the effects you can achieve.

From these early experiments you can progress to making more precise designs, though with tie-dye and to a certain degree with batik there is nearly always an element of chance in the result. When you have mastered the various techniques, you can with confidence move on to a more complete design. This can be transfer printed, painted, sprayed or dyed and afterwards given highlights or emphasis with stitchery or beads. The various methods of quilting can also be used very successfully to add texture, or to reinforce certain elements of the design.

Another aspect to consider is the painting

1 *'John's Companion' by Fée Canning: a
freely painted embroidery on calico with a
stitched foreground and with Cretan stitch
emphasizing some areas*

or dyeing of only part of the work; a piece of
canvaswork can have selected areas left free of
stitchery which can be painted or sprayed (see
colour plate 5). Some of your experiments can
be used for appliqué or patchwork. Often
parts of an otherwise uninteresting piece can
be cut out and used very successfully. Transparent fabrics such as net, chiffon, organdie,
organza or georgette can be applied to some
areas of a dyed or painted background to
alter the tone, or can even cover it completely (2). This has the effect, of course, of
totally changing the colour. Try different
transparent fabrics over some of your less
successful experiments. Very often a so-called
failure can be reassessed and used in this way.

It is also worthwhile isolating different
parts of the dyed fabric to evaluate their
potential. This can be done with a window

mount, i.e. a piece of paper or card with a rectangular hole cut in it, through which you can view selected areas. An alternative is to cut two separate L-shaped pieces of card which can be formed into a rectangle and moved around to give a number of different-sized shapes in which to isolate and reassess a design (3a,b).

General hints

1 Cover the working surfaces with several layers of newspaper or a sheet of polythene.

2 Try to keep the working area clean, tidy and organized.

3 Wipe up any spills straightaway, and wash and clean all equipment immediately after use.

4 Check the fibre content of the fabric to be used (see Appendix I, page 126).

5 Wash or boil all new fabrics, particularly if they are to be worn or washed after use. Many contain a dressing which will prevent the penetration and the evenness of the dye.

6 Keep a record of your experiments.

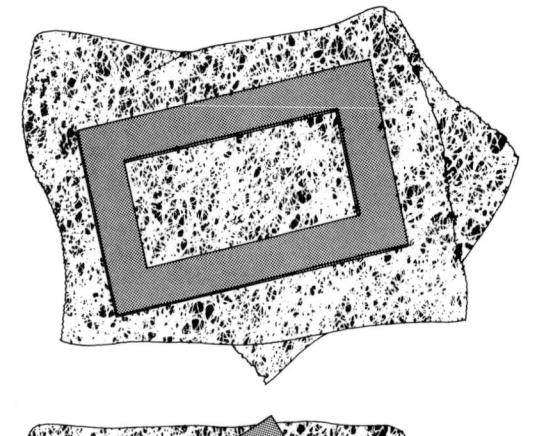

a

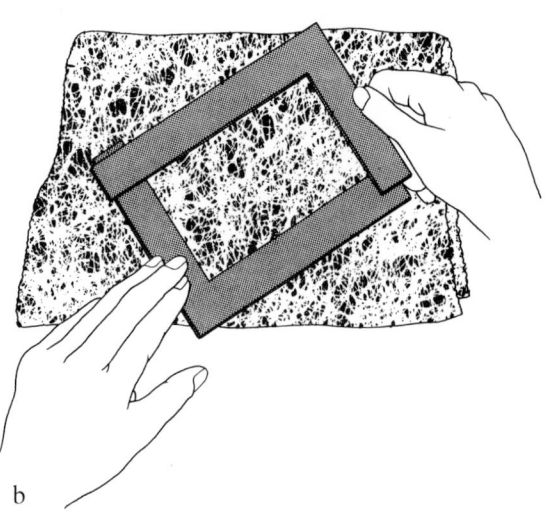

b

2 *This striking batik portrait, 'The Seductress' by Pepa Santamaria, shows the application of net, creating shadows and differences in tone; free machining outlines the features and simple hand stitches are used for the head-dress and necklace*

3 (a) *Window mount in card used to isolate selected areas of a design or a piece of dyed fabric*

(b) *L-shaped cards can be moved closer together or further apart to give smaller or larger enclosed areas*

3 TIE-DYE

Tie-dyeing is a resist process whereby fabric is folded and tied up in a variety of ways. It is then plunged into either hot or cold dyes, and those areas most tightly bound, or in the centre of the bundle, will resist the penetration of colour. Whilst a certain amount of chance determines the finished result – exact repetition is impossible to achieve – a range of similar effects can be reproduced by repeating a prescribed method. Of course, the number of ways of folding and tying the fabric are limitless and experimentation is necessary. After the first dyeing, the sample can be dried and, if desired, folded and retied in a different way. If it is then dyed another colour, a four-colour sample will be produced. For example, if the background colour is white and the first dye is red, the result will be a two-colour design in red and white. If you then refold, retie and dye it in blue, some areas will still remain red and white, others will be blue and the rest will be purple, i.e. red and blue.

General equipment

Most of the equipment needed for experiments in tie-dye is readily available. Before you begin, cover the working surfaces with plastic or several layers of old newspapers, and for the actual dyeing, wear rubber gloves and protective clothing.

A plastic or enamel container. This is needed for cold-water dyes and should be large enough to hold sufficient water in which to submerge totally the article to be dyed. An upright container such as a bucket is generally the most useful, although a shallow bowl is necessary for some methods if you do not wish to fold or crease the article further.

A heat-resistant container. For hot-water dyes a stainless steel or enamel bucket is necessary, or a large saucepan.

A measuring jug and bowl.

Plastic teaspoons and tablespoons. These are useful for measuring and stirring the dye.

A kettle.

4 *'Window with Plants': a three-dimensional appliqué panel by the author; the sky is of marbled tie-dyed cotton, the field tritik gathered; areas of shadow are achieved by bonding on a very fine net. The plant arrangement in the foreground has machine stitched padded leaves in silk with off-cuts of batik 'crackle' fabric giving a delicate veined appearance to the leaves of the climbing plant.* (Courtesy Mr and Mrs A Spivak)

5 *Needleweaving and needle-lace stitches produce a tree-shape in this circular panel. Picot leaves, eyelets and raised cup stitch provide the foreground texture and a tie-dyed fabric placed behind adds colour to the all-white embroidery*

Equipment for tying

Threads and yarns. Almost any thread can be used for tying up the fabric. Try tying with the following; string of all thicknesses, cotton or linen thread, cord, raffia, ribbon and tape, rubber bands. Generally it is more difficult to tie-dye a heavy fabric successfully if it has been tied with a fine thread, and a thick string may prove too much of a resist on a fine fabric.

Polythene and mesh bags and old net curtains. These are useful for the marbling technique.

Dowels and pieces of hardboard or plywood. Some of the folded and tied methods require the use of these.

Miscellaneous objects. A selection of bottle-tops, buttons, cotton-reels, shells, pebbles or rice can be tied up in your chosen way and will leave an interesting imprint. It is essential to use a cold-water dye for this particular type of experiment.

Equipment for clamping

Bulldog clips, paper clips and clothes pegs. These provide a quick way of securing a bundle satisfactorily, particularly for folded experiments. Clothes pegs should preferably be of the plastic variety, as wooden ones take the colour of the dye so can only be used once. Plastic pegs can only be used in cold-water dyes. Paper clips and bulldog clips rust very quickly so should be dried thoroughly immediately after use.

Fabrics

Use old cotton or linen sheeting for experiments. It needs no preparation provided that it is clean. New fabrics should be washed thoroughly, by boiling if necessary. Check that the material is suitable for dyeing – many fabrics have been commercially finished with a dressing which prevents a deep and even dye.

Natural fibres

These can be dyed in hot- or cold-water dyes and include:

Cotton – lawn, poplin, calico, muslin, towelling, cambric, voile, flannelette, velvet, velveteen, corduroy.

Linen – fine or heavy, and linen scrim.

Silk – shantung, raw silk, wild silk, chiffon and georgette.

Wool – most wools will dye, and contrary to popular belief can be used with both hot- and cold-water dyes, provided that care is taken

not to subject the fabric to sudden extremes of temperature.

Man-made and synthetic fibres

These fall into several groups which react in different ways and need different treatments. (See Appendices I and II, pages 126, 127).

Acetates – Tricel. Use hot-water dyes.

Acrylics – Acrilan, Courtelle, Dralon, Orlon. These will not dye satisfactorily.

Polyesters – Crimplene, Dacron, Terylene, Trevira. Only hot-water dyes are suitable and will result in pale shades only.

Polyamides – Nylon, Enkalon, Celon. For good results you need hot-water dyes.

Viscose rayons – Evlan, Vincel. Good results can be achieved with hot- or cold-water dyes.

Dyes

The dyes described are those most readily available and the easiest to use. For suppliers, see page 129.

Cold-water dyes

Cold-water dyes are generally faster than hot-water dyes to washing and light.

Dylon Cold-water dyes

These are widely available and quick and easy to use. They come in a wide range of colours which can also be mixed together for an even greater number of shades.

For 200–250 g (6–8 oz) dry-weight fabric/2–3 sq m (2–3 sq yd) medium-weight fabric (NB: the dyebath will only remain stable for two to three hours after the salt and soda have been added):

1 Dissolve the dye powder in 0.5 litre (1 pint) warm water. Stir well.

2 Add this solution to the dyebath into which you have put enough cold water to cover the article. Stir well.

3 Dissolve 4 tablespoonsful of salt and 1 tablespoonful of household soda in 0.5 litre (1 pint) of very hot water; stir well, making sure it has completely dissolved.

4 Add salt and soda solution to the dyebath and stir well.

5 Very carefully immerse the thoroughly wetted article. Stir gently for the first ten minutes, then at intervals, keeping the fabric submerged until the dyeing is complete – up to one hour.

6 Remove from the dyebath and rinse thoroughly in cold water several times.

7 Wash with hot water to remove any residue of dye and rinse again in cold.

8 Untie the sample carefully. If it has been tied very tightly with a fine thread, it may be necessary to cut the bindings with scissors. Proceed with caution so as not to damage the fabric.

9 Rinse once again. Dry and iron.

NB: For wool, in place of salt and soda use 1½ cups of vinegar, immerse in hot water instead of cold and rinse in warm water.

Procion M. dyes

Procion M. dyes have been developed by I.C.I. and are obtainable from specialist craft shops. These cold-water dyes are a little more complicated to use than the Dylon ones, but there is a good range of bright, fast colours. If you are willing to experiment, the dyes can be intermixed and used in differing quantities to produce a wide range of shades and colours.

For 200–250 g (6–8 oz) dry-weight fabric/2–3 sq m (2–3 sq yd) medium-weight fabric (NB: the dyebath will only remain stable for 2–3 hours after the salt and soda have been added):

1 In a large bowl, mix 1–3 teaspoonsful of dye to a smooth paste with a little cold water, making sure there are no lumps.

2 In a measuring jug, dissolve 2 level tablespoonsful of urea in 0.5 litre (1 pint) lukewarm water. Add this to the dye paste and stir well.

3 Rinse the measuring jug and in it dissolve 4 tablespoonsful of household salt in 0.5 litre (1 pint) very hot water. Stir well and add to dye solution.

4 Add this solution to a dyebath containing enough cold water to cover the fabric to be dyed. Stir well.

5 Immerse the previously wetted article very carefully in the dyebath, and leave for six minutes, stirring gently and continuously.

6 In the measuring jug, dissolve 1 level tablespoonful of washing soda in a little warm water.

7 Remove the fabric from the dyebath. Add soda solution to the dyebath and stir thoroughly.

8 Immediately return the fabric to the dyebath and leave for between 15 and 45 minutes, depending on the strength of colour required. Stir occasionally.

9 Remove the fabric from the dyebath.

10 If redyeing in another colour, untie, rinse thoroughly in cold water and leave to dry. For one dyeing or for the final dye, do not rinse but leave to dry in a warm place for 24 hours. Then untie and rinse off in cold water and dry again.

Hot-water dyes

Dylon Multi-purpose dyes

There is a wide range of colours to choose from, particularly for dark shades.

For 250 g (8 oz) dry-weight fabric/2–3 sq m (2–3 sq yd) medium-weight fabric:

1 Dissolve the powder in 0.5 litre (1 pint) boiling water. Stir well.

2 Add the solution to enough cold water to cover the fabric in a heat-resistant vessel.

6 *Marbling: this example of heavy cotton deeply dyed shows an entirely different result from figure 4, in which the marbled sky was lightly dipped in a pale colour*

23

3 Add 1 tablespoonful of salt. Stir well.

4 Wet article thoroughly and immerse. Stir well.

5 Heat to simmer and maintain for 20 minutes, stirring gently to keep article submerged.

6 Rinse thoroughly.

NB: For wool, bring slowly to simmer and reduce heat at once. Stir very gently for ten minutes. Rinse in warm water, and do not subject the fabric to extremes of hot and cold water.

Dylon Liquid Instant Fabric dyes

These are available in a small range of the most popular colours of the Dylon Multi-purpose Hot-Water dyes. As they come ready-mixed in plastic bottles and need only the addition of salt, they are very quick to use and convenient for both small and large amounts of fabric.

For 125–150 g (4–5 oz) dry weight fabric/ 1–1·5 sq m (1–1·5 sq yd), use 1 capful of dye plus 1 tablespoonful of salt:

1 Shake the bottle well before use.

2 Fill a heat-resistant vessel with enough very hot water to cover the fabric to be dyed and to allow free movement whilst dyeing.

3 Add the dye and salt. Stir well.

4 Very carefully immerse the thoroughly wet-

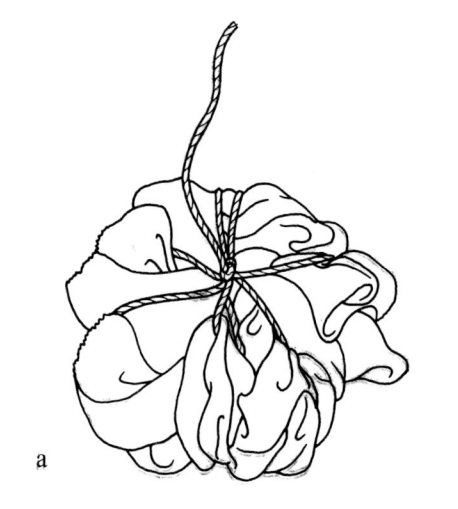

a

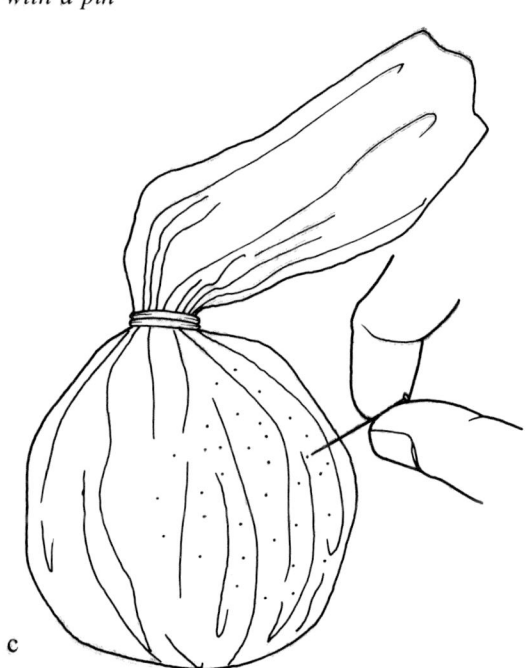

7 Marbling: (a) Method 1, crumpled and tied up with string
(b) Method 2, using a plastic mesh bag
(c) Method 3, using polythene bags pricked with a pin

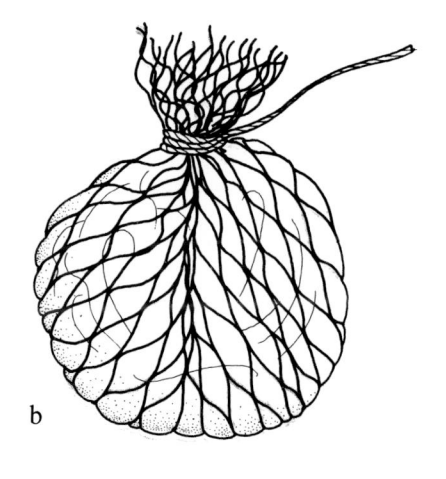

b

c

24

ted article. Keep submerged and simmer for 15–20 minutes (for wool ten minutes).

5 Remove from dyebath and rinse thoroughly.

Methods

Marbling

Of the many methods of tie-dye, marbling is the simplest and makes a random variegated pattern **(6)**.

Crumple a piece of fabric up in your hand and use one of the following ways to secure it **(7a–c)**.

The first method entails tying the fabric firmly with string, cord, raffia, tape, strong thread or rubber bands, with the bindings criss-crossing over the entire surface. Alternatively, place the bundle in a plastic mesh bag (the type used for vegetables and fruit). Twist the opening round to make as small a bundle as possible and secure with string or rubber bands. Additional string or rubber bands may be used, crossing over the bundle to hold it firm. Open mesh fabrics such as old net curtains can also be used. The third method is to place the bundle in a polythene bag, closing it very securely as before. Put into a second polythene bag and fasten with string or rubber bands round the top. Prick all over with a pin.

With all these methods, do experiment with the way you actually crumple the fabric – from the middle outwards, or from side to side. Each will achieve a slightly different effect. Remember that the fabric on the outside of the bundle will be brighter than the inside, where the dye is less likely to penetrate. If you wet the bundle thoroughly after you have tied it up, then drain it before immersing it in the dye, you will get a better resist and therefore more contrast between dyed areas.

Folding

Fabric can be folded or pleated in innumerable ways before binding and clamping. This method is useful for repeat motifs, overall patterns or single motifs.

At its simplest, if a piece of fabric is folded in half and then bound or clamped, it will result in a mirror image when dyed **(8a)**.

If the fabric is folded in half and half again the other way, then the design will be quartered **(8b)**. Fabric can also be folded in concertina form **(8c)**.

It is important to remember when folding that the fabric on the inside will be least likely to take the dye. Therefore, if you wish the

8 *Folding: (a) Folding in half for a mirror image*
(b) Folding in four for a quartered design
(c) Concertina fold

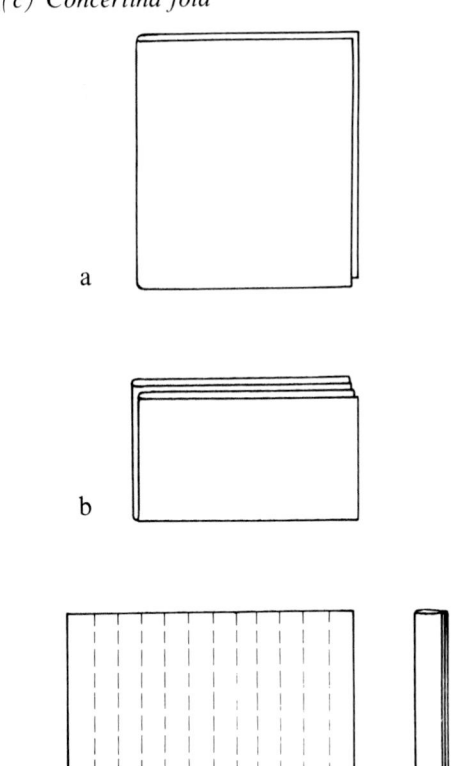

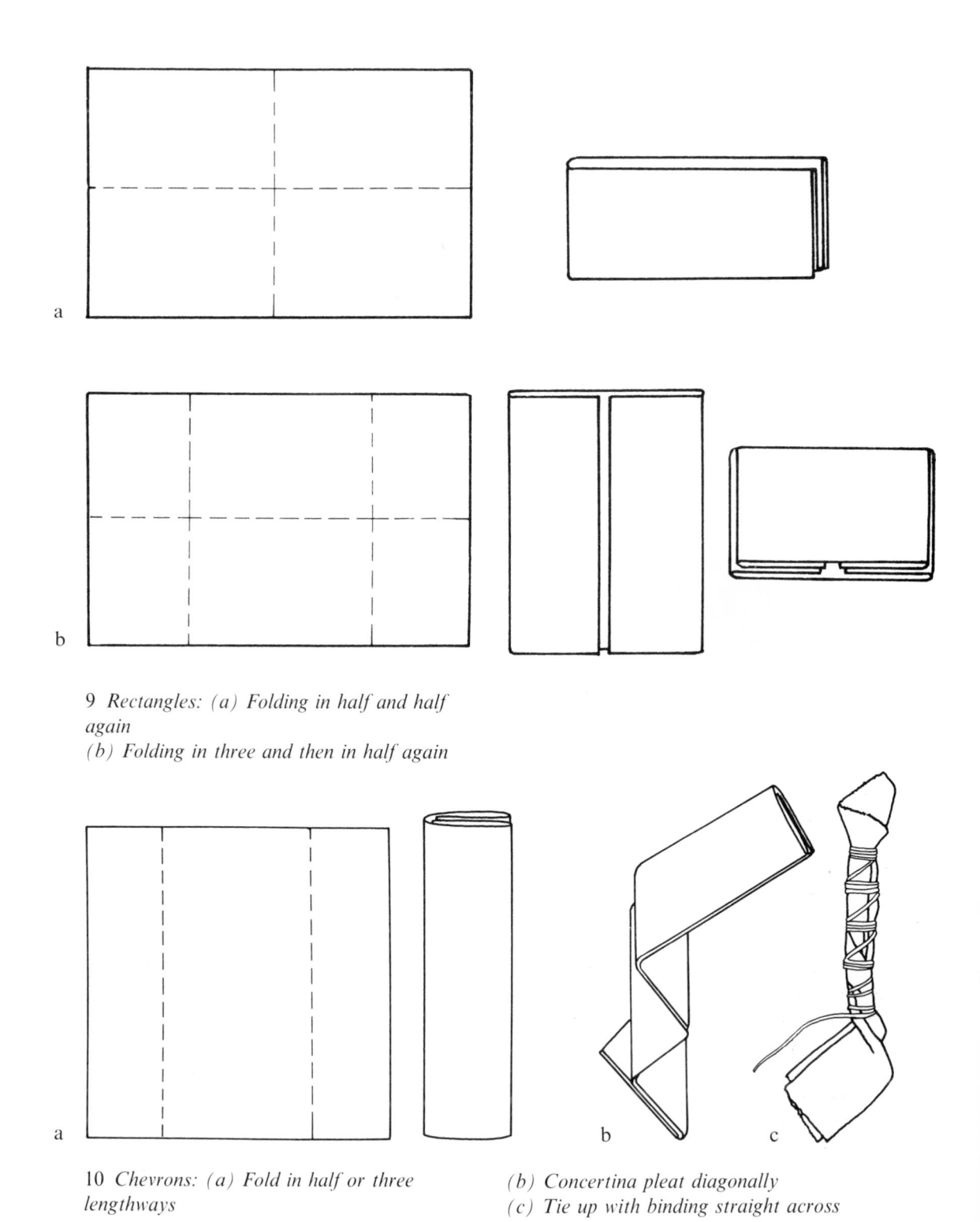

9 *Rectangles: (a) Folding in half and half again*
(b) Folding in three and then in half again

10 *Chevrons: (a) Fold in half or three lengthways*

(b) Concertina pleat diagonally
(c) Tie up with binding straight across

central area of a piece of work to be darkest in colour, then it should remain towards the outside of the folded bundle.

Rectangles
Fold rectangles in half or into three lengthways, then across (9a,b). Bind with regular rows of similar yarns. Also experiment on another sample with different thicknesses of thread, string, ribbon etc. to achieve narrow and wide stripes of resist. Try concertina pleating both on the straight grain of the fabric and diagonally. For chevrons, fold the cloth in half lengthways, concertina pleat diagonally and bind as above for stripes (10a–c). For double or more chevrons, fold the sample lengthways into four or more thicknesses and proceed as above (11).

11 *Chevrons: white linen randomly tied with heavy string and dyed in a dark green hot-water dye produces a distinct zigzag pattern*

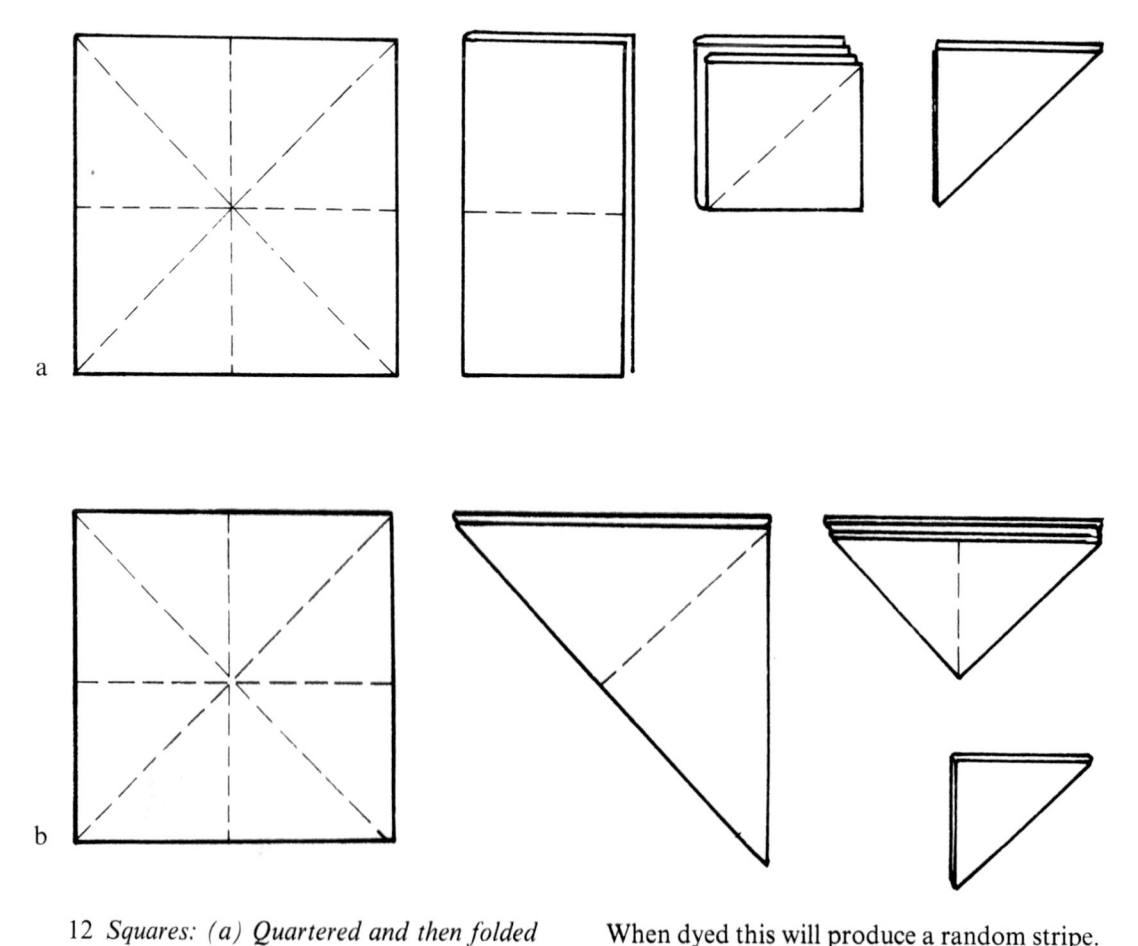

12 *Squares: (a) Quartered and then folded diagonally into a triangle*
(b) Folded in quarters and then in half again to produce a small triangle

Squares

Squares of fabric can be folded in the same way as rectangles. A square can also be quartered and then folded diagonally into a triangle, or it can be folded in half diagonally and then into quarters diagonally (12a,b).

Clamping

Pegs, paper clips and bulldog clips all hold the folded fabric very firmly and produce good results (13). For your first experiment, fold the fabric in half and gather it up into a long bundle; place clothes pegs along both edges.

When dyed this will produce a random stripe. For a more controlled stripe the fabric should be concertina pleated instead of being gathered up before clamping (14). Experiment with the different folding methods on both squares and rectangles of fabric. Try clamping, dyeing, untying and then reclamping and redyeing a second colour. Clamps are also useful to hold a bundle or folded sample temporarily in place before binding.

Binding

The same folded methods can also be bound with yarn or rubber bands. If you are using yarn or string, start by catching the end of the thread in your first few rows of binding, and finish it with a slip knot (15). This makes it easy to undo after dyeing.

28

13 Tie-dyeing: this square of fabric has been
quartered as in figure 12a and secured with
bulldog clips to make the light rectangular
areas

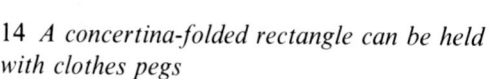

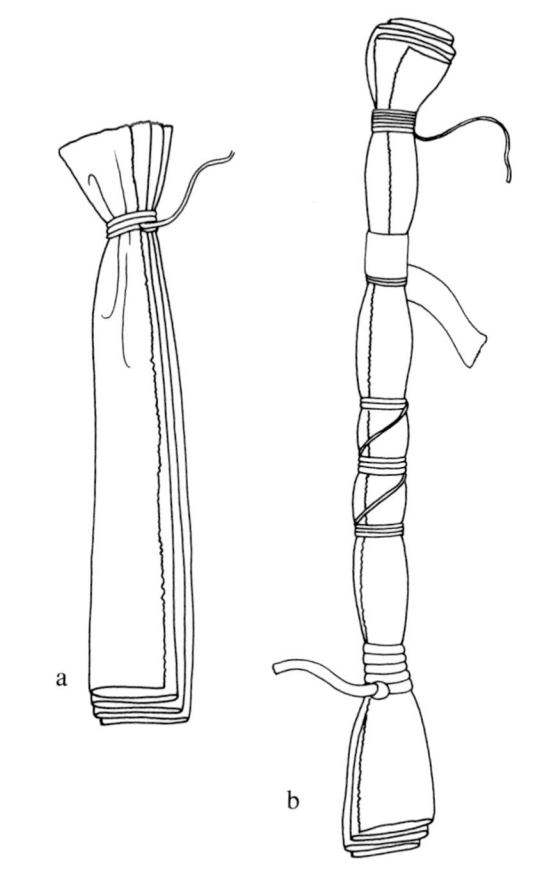

14 *A concertina-folded rectangle can be held with clothes pegs*

15 *Binding: (a) Begin by catching the end of the string in the first few rows of binding (b) Experiment with different ways of binding, using a selection of string, cord or tape; finish with a slip knot*

Dowels, sticks and hardboard shapes

The use of these produces some very unusual effects which lend themselves very well to enhancement with embroidery.

For the dowel or stick method, either gather or concertina pleat the sample into a narrow length. Wind this diagonally around the length of the dowel and bind straight across along the entire length with your chosen yarn **(16)**. Dye, rinse and untie before drying.

The hardboard (or plywood) method involves placing the folded sample between two identical slats (lollipop sticks will do for small trials) and either clamping together with bull-dog clips or binding with string **(19a)**. More exciting and unexpected results can be achieved if you have two pieces of hardboard or plywood cut into identical irregular shapes and sandwich the fabric between them. Clamp

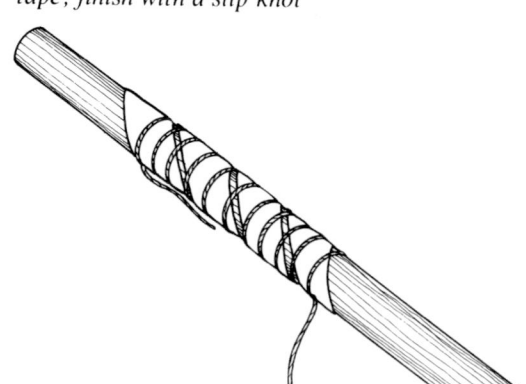

16 *Dowels: wind a length of fabric or tape diagonally around the length of the dowel and bind straight across; this will produce a chevron or diagonal design*

17 *Close-up of the canvas footstool illustrated in colour plate 1. The suede leaves have been tie-dyed using the dowel method* **(16)**

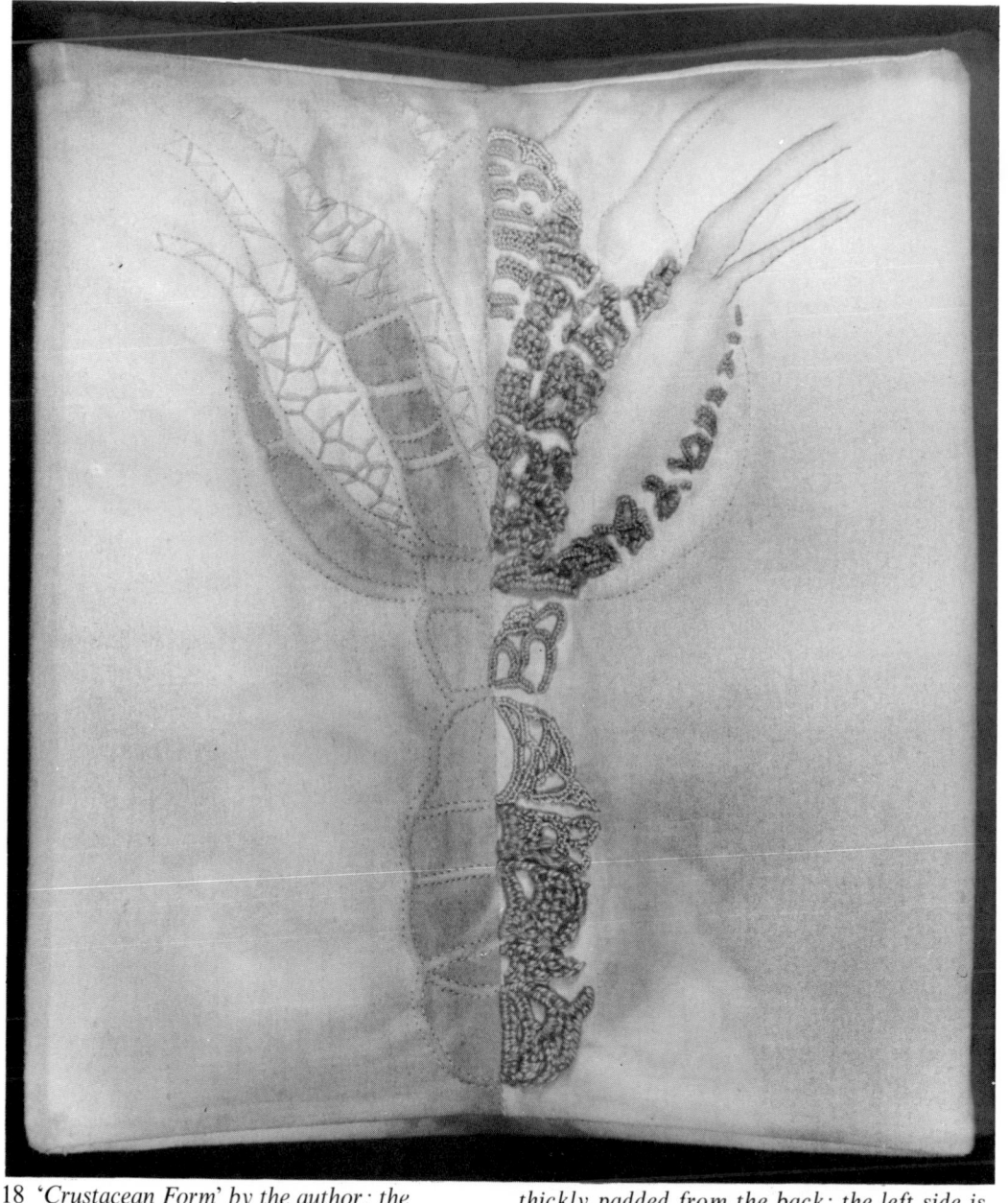

18 'Crustacean Form' by the author; the fabric is tie-dyed by the hardboard method **(18b)**. The pattern emerging from the experimental dyeing evoked a reflected crustacean form; the right-hand side is boldly stitched with crochet and cotton perle, and thickly padded from the back; the left side is more delicately stitched with Italian quilting and buttonhole bars in fine thread re-iterating the shape. The two sides are mounted facing each other at an angle on a fabric-covered wooden framework

32

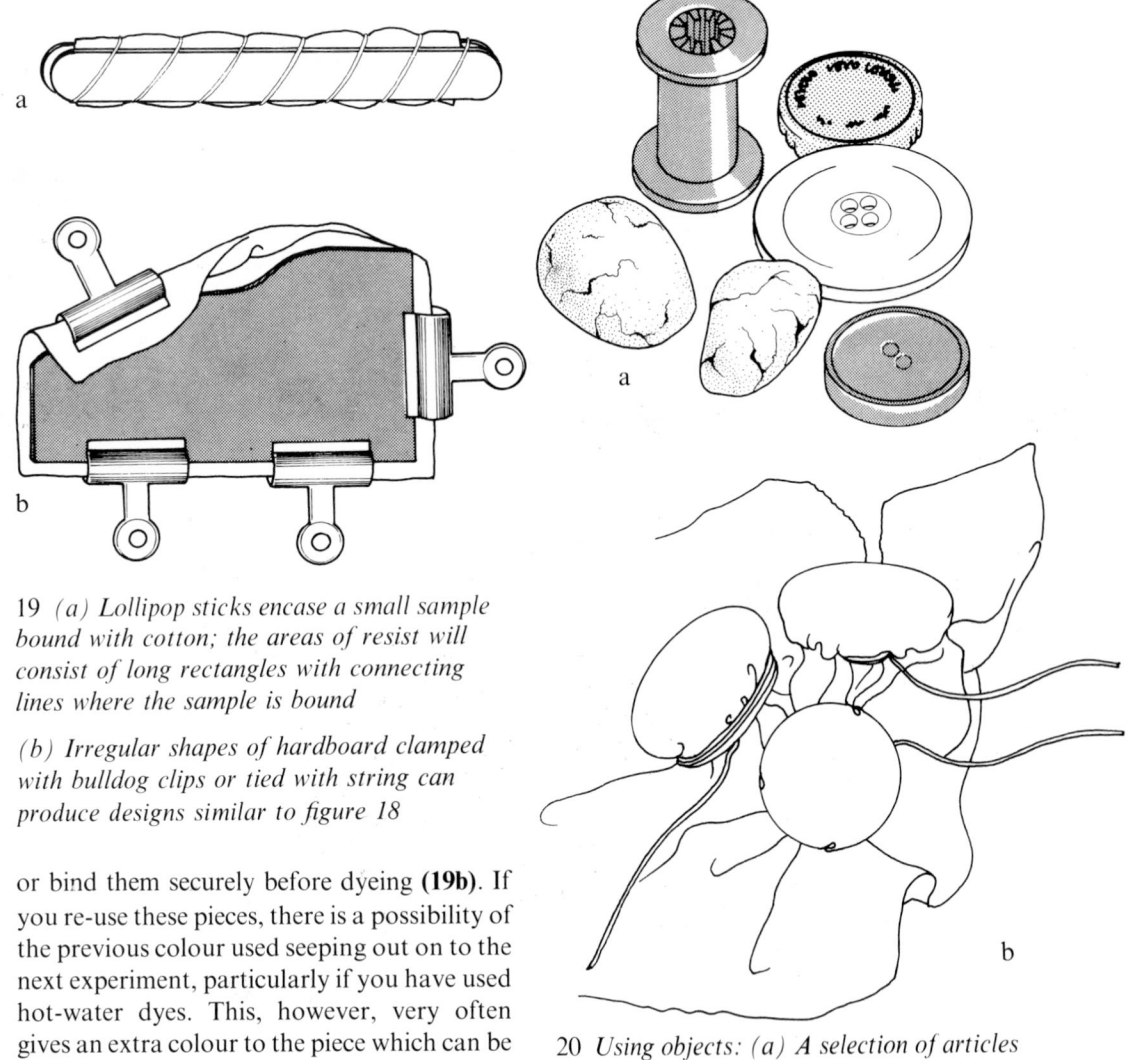

19 *(a) Lollipop sticks encase a small sample bound with cotton; the areas of resist will consist of long rectangles with connecting lines where the sample is bound*

(b) Irregular shapes of hardboard clamped with bulldog clips or tied with string can produce designs similar to figure 18

or bind them securely before dyeing **(19b)**. If you re-use these pieces, there is a possibility of the previous colour used seeping out on to the next experiment, particularly if you have used hot-water dyes. This, however, very often gives an extra colour to the piece which can be an unexpected bonus **(18)**.

Using objects

All sorts of articles, such as pebbles, stones, shells, bottle tops, buttons and cotton reels can be placed in a sample of single or folded fabric and either bound with yarn or secured with a number of rubber bands **(20a,b)**. This method usually results in a series of circular motifs of different qualities and sizes. Interesting pieces can be made by repeating the process with the object tied in other areas of

20 *Using objects: (a) A selection of articles suitable for tying up*
(b) Secure them in the fabric with string or yarn

the design after the first dyeing **(21)**. It is advisable to plan the positioning of the objects before beginning. Mark their positions with a soft pencil. You will then be able to see exactly where each object should be placed, even though as you proceed with the binding the fabric will become distorted. Dye in cold-water dyes, rinse and dry.

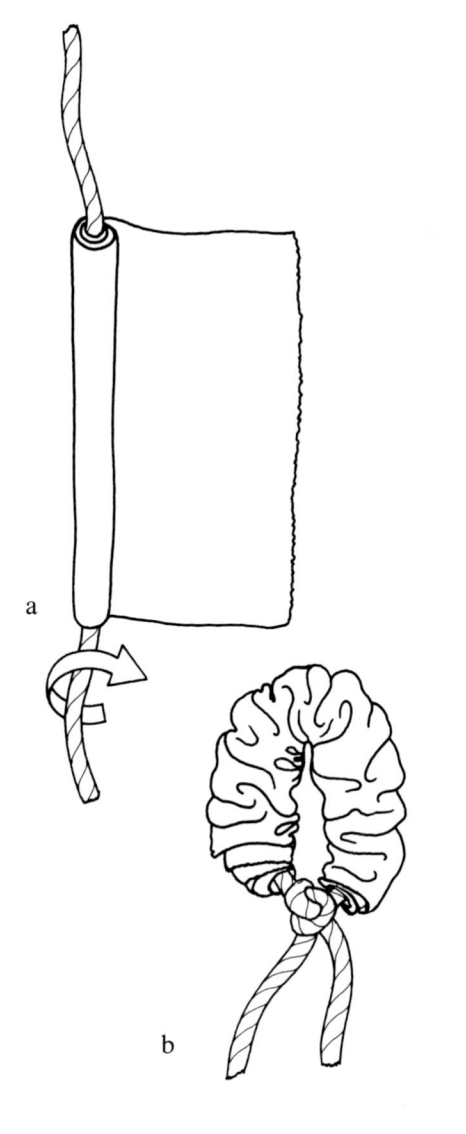

a

b

Rolling over a cord

This method results in a mottled effect, with the inside of the roll pale and the outside darker. Fine fabrics such as lawn, muslin or chiffon are best. Take a thick cord, longer than the width of the fabric, and place it along one side of the sample. Roll it across, covering with the fabric as you go until you have a long roll. Fold this in half and, holding the two ends of the cord together, push up the fabric towards the top until you have as small a bundle as possible. Tie the ends of the cord together (**22a,b**). The bundle can either be bound or left as it is. Dye, rinse and untie. For an all-over mottled effect it will be necessary to reroll, starting from the other side, and dye again. This technique can also be used diagonally starting at one corner and rolling towards the opposite one (**23**). If the fabric is folded in two and the rolling finished with the fold on the outside, the central area of the sample will be the darkest.

Tritik

Tritik, from the Malay word meaning 'droplet', is a method of resist dyeing which is a development of tie-dye. In this technique, instead of binding or clamping, the resist is achieved with the use of needle and strong thread. Tiny dots or 'droplets' can be sewn or bound; the fabric can be pleated, tucked, oversewn or gathered, and the thread pulled very tight. The domestic sewing machine can also be used for these methods – a zig-zag stitch and gathering both produce very good resists. The stitches are fairly easy to unpick with sharp scissors or a stitch-ripper, after dyeing. In this way, patterns and defined shapes can result. The fabric and dyes suitable are the same as those described for tie-dye. The material can be used either folded for repeat patterns or singly. Experiment first with fine fabric such as lawn or muslin.

Gathering

Use strong thread, such as button thread or

22 Rolling over a cord: (a) Roll up the fabric over a thick cord either straight or diagonally (**23**)
(b) Push up the fabric into a small bundle and tie the ends of the cord together

21 Opposite *Using objects: a striking example showing the effect of using a variety of different sizes and shapes of buttons and stones. After the first dyebath of yellow, the objects were repositioned and retied before dyeing in dark brown*

23 *Rolling over a cord: in this example the fabric has been rolled diagonally, giving a mottled, snakeskin appearance*

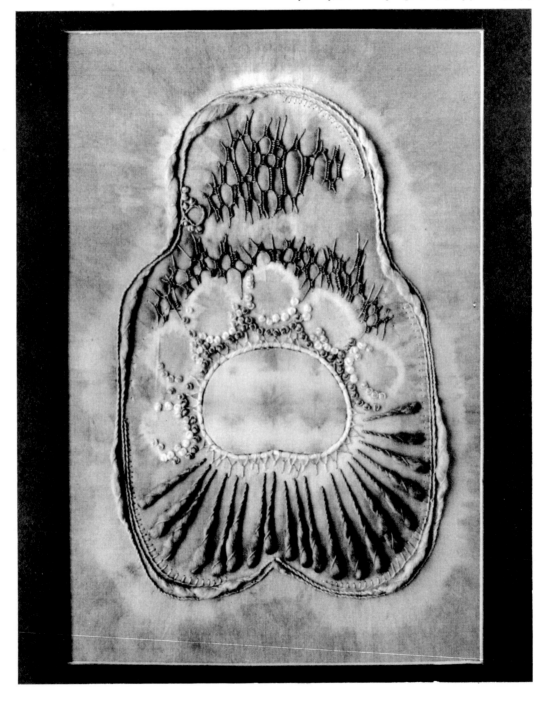

24 'Pepper' by Moria Grafton; a tritik work
with additional stitching in needle weaving,
French knots and couching. See also figure 45

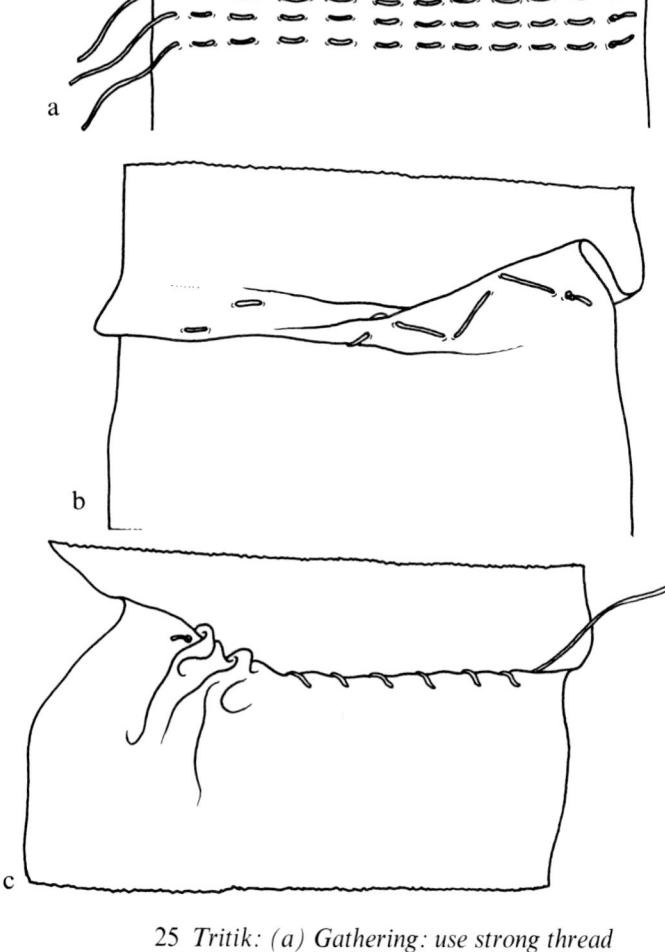

with each other with differing distances between each row. Do not draw up the gathers until all the running stitches are completed. Then pull the thread tightly and fasten off securely. A row of stitches in zig-zag formation gives an interesting effect.

Tucks

Make tucks across the width of the fabric and stitch through both layers with several rows of even stitches (25b). These rows can either be sewn directly below each other or the stitches alternated. Tucks produce alternate stripes of dark and light when dyed. Gather up the threads as before when all the stitching is done.

Oversewing

This will produce a narrow textured line. Fold the fabric along the line of the design and sew over the fold. Pull up the stitches a little as you sew, as it is difficult to do so later (25c).

Outlines

Draw the outline of the design on the fabric in soft pencil or water-erasable pen. Run two parallel lines of tiny stitches either side of this line (27a). Pull the thread tight and fasten off securely. If the design is symmetrical, the fabric can be folded in two and the stitches taken through the double layer. Do not attempt too small a design or lines which are close together, as there will not be enough definition after dyeing. A zig-zag machined line will give a very good resist through several layers of fabric and need not be gathered up.

Dots

Small dots can be made with the tritik method, although it is better not to pass the

25 *Tritik: (a) Gathering: use strong thread and sew with running stitches*
(b) Tucks: these can be stitched as illustrated with a zig-zag stitch or using straight rows of running stitch, either even or random
(c) Oversewing: this can be done as illustrated or with the stitches closer together for a more distinct line of resist

gimp, and start with a knot at the end. Sew with running stitches along a previously drawn line (25a). Do several experiments with different length stitches until you get the effect you require. Stitch a number of rows parallel

26 *Tritik sample showing zig-zag tucks, oversewing on a pleat and gathering. The ribbons and trimmings were dyed at the same time as the background fabric, but for differing lengths of time to produce a selection of shades*

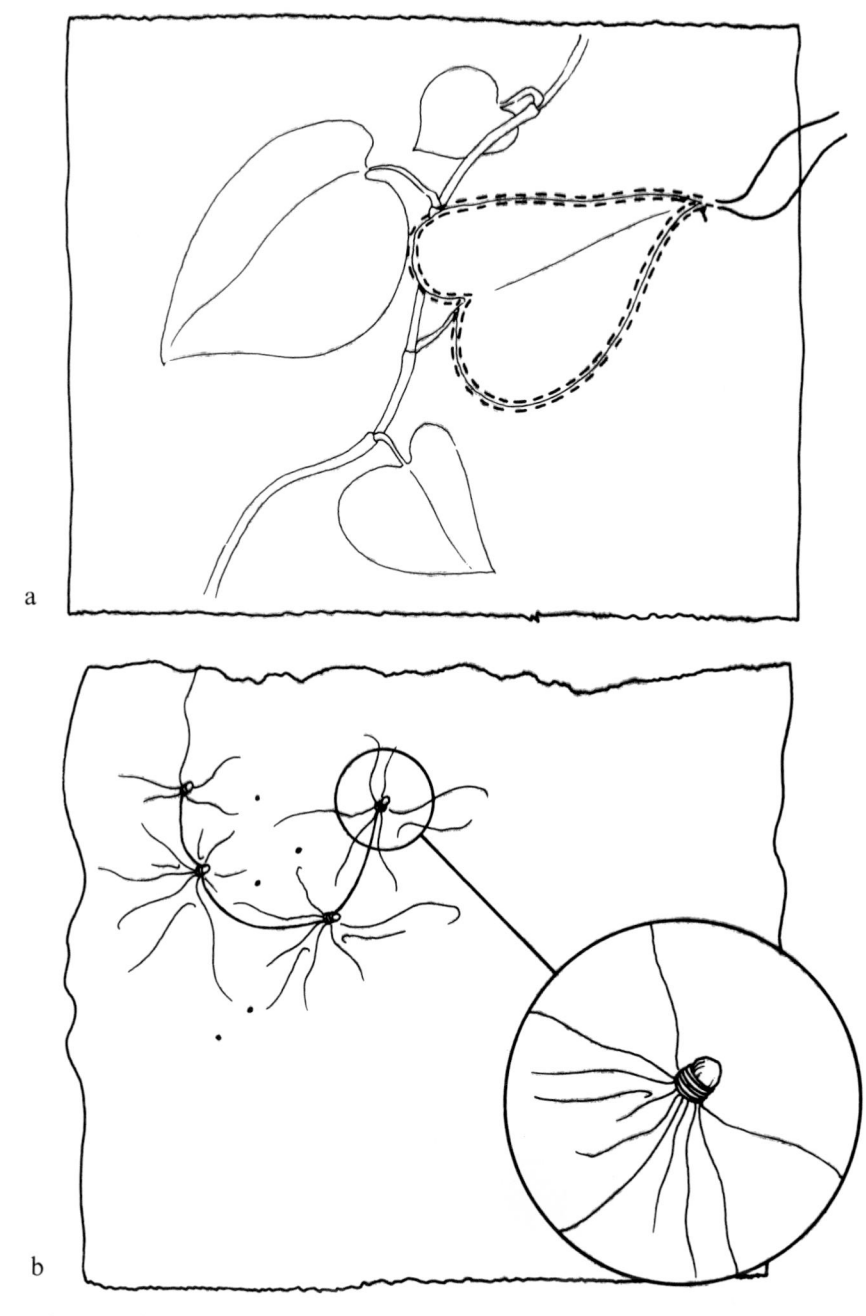

27 *(a) Outlines: a double row of tiny*
gathering stitches is sewn in strong thread
(b) Dots: tiny dots or circles can be tied
round with fine cotton thread. Make sure that
the design is clearly marked on the fabric
before beginning

40

needle through the fabric except to begin and fasten off (**27b**). Mark the dots on the fabric before you begin. This is essential unless it is a random sample, as it is impossible to judge where the next dot should be once the binding has begun. Pick up the point of the dot between your forefinger and thumb and wind fine thread tightly round, finishing with a slip knot. This is much easier to do if the yarn is threaded through a needle. Then move on to the next dot and proceed as before. This technique is simple to undo after dyeing, as all you need to do is to hold either edge of the fabric and tug outwards – the thread will be pulled off the point of each dot. The fabric can be used either single or double. It can also be slightly dampened before you start, which prevents it from slipping.

Ombré and part dyeing

Although this is not strictly a tie-dye method, fabrics partially dyed and those shaded from dark to light are useful additions to your selection of dyed materials. The technique also gives good practice in achieving an evenly dyed result.

Ombré, or *shaded dyeing*, can be done in monochrome or two or more colours. Use a cold-water dye in a dark hue and wear rubber gloves. The fabric can be immersed in one of the following ways (**28a–c**).

For the first method, thoroughly wet the fabric and, holding it between the forefinger and thumb of both hands, lower it gently into the dye. Immediately begin to withdraw it very slowly, moving it to and fro. This should take about 10–15 minutes. It is very important not to allow it to remain in one position for any length of time as a line will result on the finished piece and you will not achieve a smooth gradation of tone. A little practice is needed to get the right degree of colour.

The second method is suitable for small pieces, not larger than the width of the dyebath. Use a shallow container and attach the fabric to a lath or dowel with drawing pins.

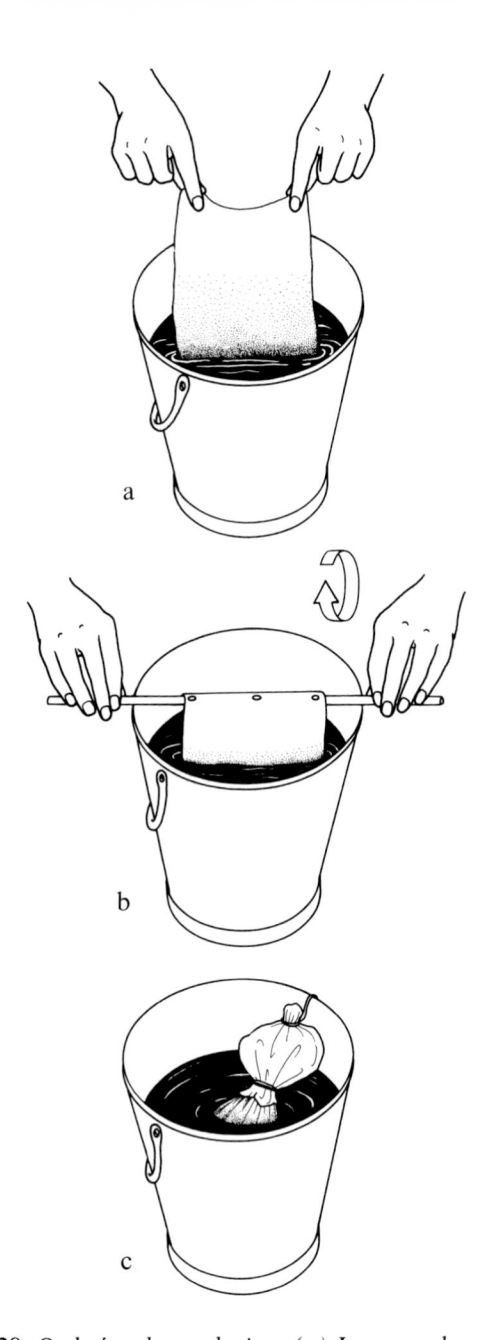

28 *Ombré and part dyeing: (a) Immerse the fabric gently in the dyebath and gradually withdraw it very slowly, moving it to and fro (b) Immerse the fabric and slowly roll it up on to the dowel, at the same time moving it to and fro (c) For part dyeing, immerse only the area to be dyed and cover the remainder of the fabric with a polythene bag firmly bound with yarn*

41

Lower the wet fabric into the dye, resting the lath on the edges of the container. Gradually roll up the fabric on to the lath, moving it to and fro. After removing the fabric from the dyebath, immediately hang it up to drip dry, with the darkest area at the bottom. When dry, rinse thoroughly and dry again. If you wish to dye the other end of the fabric another colour, do not dry it but immediately repeat the process in another pre-mixed dyebath. Where the two dyes overlap you will obtain a third colour. For example, if one end is yellow and the other blue, then the two colours in the middle will combine to produce green.

For *part dyeing* (i.e. if just a portion of the fabric is to be dyed) place a polythene bag over the area to remain undyed and bind it very tightly with string round the top. Only allow the uncovered fabric to be immersed in the dye. If possible tie the sample either to the handle of the dyebath, or suspend it from something above. For example, you can rest a lath or piece of wood across the top of the container and tie the sample to this with just the area to be dyed dipped in the liquid. When the dyeing period is complete, take the fabric from the dyebath and, before removing the polythene bag, rinse the dyed area thoroughly.

Discharge dyeing

This is a reversal of the technique of tie-dye, which means that the colour in the fabric is expelled, or discharged, except where it has been tied or clamped. This will, in fact, give a positive image instead of the negative one which normal tie-dyeing produces. For example, with ordinary tie-dye you would have a white design on a red background, whilst with the discharge method it would be red on white (**29**). Use fabrics which are not colour-fast, including those which have previously been dyed in hot-water dyes. Test commercially dyed fabrics to see if the colour can be bleached out. Proprietary brands of colour and stain remover can be used, following the

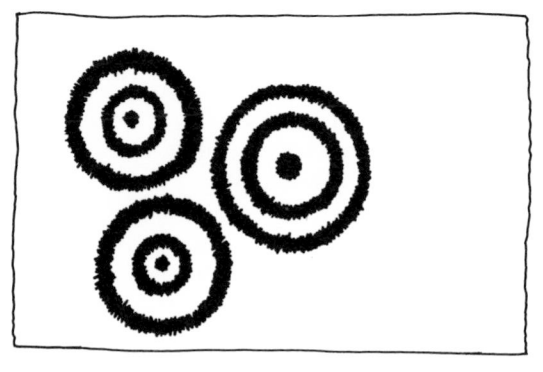

29 *Negative images (top) are produced by tie-dyeing three circular motifs. The positive images (below) are achieved by discharge dyeing a similar design, i.e. the colour is bleached from the background but remains in those areas which have been bound*

makers' instructions. Alternatively, make up a weak solution of one part household bleach to six parts water and immerse the sample in this until the colour is discharged.

Dyeing threads

Threads and yarns of most types can be dyed to match or contrast with dyed fabric. They can, of course, also be specially dyed to complement a background of commercially printed or dyed material. Hot- and cold-water dyes of the type used for tie-dye are suitable, depending on the fibre of the yarn (see Appendix II, page 127). It is best to wind the threads into a skein or cut them into manageable

lengths, secured together with another thread tied in a half hitch knot. This thread can then be held in order to lower the skein into the dye, and can be tied to the handle of the dyebath or to a lath resting across the top of the vessel. If several types of yarn are being immersed together, it is best to keep them separate in this way to prevent them becoming entangled. Dissimilar yarns will all take up the dye to a different extent to give a variety of shades. Threads can also be space-dyed **(30)**. This is a tie-dye method in which the skein is tightly bound at either even or random intervals to produce a two-colour shaded yarn. The process can be repeated, by retying and redyeing in another colour, for a multi-coloured result.

Fine fabrics, such as chiffon, nylon and voile, can be cut or torn into narrow strips and treated in this way. They can then be used for couching down or for stitching through a loosely woven background **(31)**. Ribbons, tapes and cords can be dyed or space-dyed to complement clothes and household items.

Experiments

The following tie-dye experiments will help you to produce a range of interesting and colourful samples, all suitable for use with a variety of embroidery techniques. Some can be used as background fabrics for panels, pictures or wallhangings. Others will create interesting patterns to cut out and use for patchwork and appliqué. Tie-dyed effects also lend themselves well to use on garments and accessories, as well as on household items such as cushions and quilts.

Marbling

This makes a marvellous background for use as sky, vegetation and underwater effects, or just as a subtle variation to add interest to an otherwise bland fabric.

For a *sky effect* use a fine fabric in white, such as muslin or lawn, and choose a pale

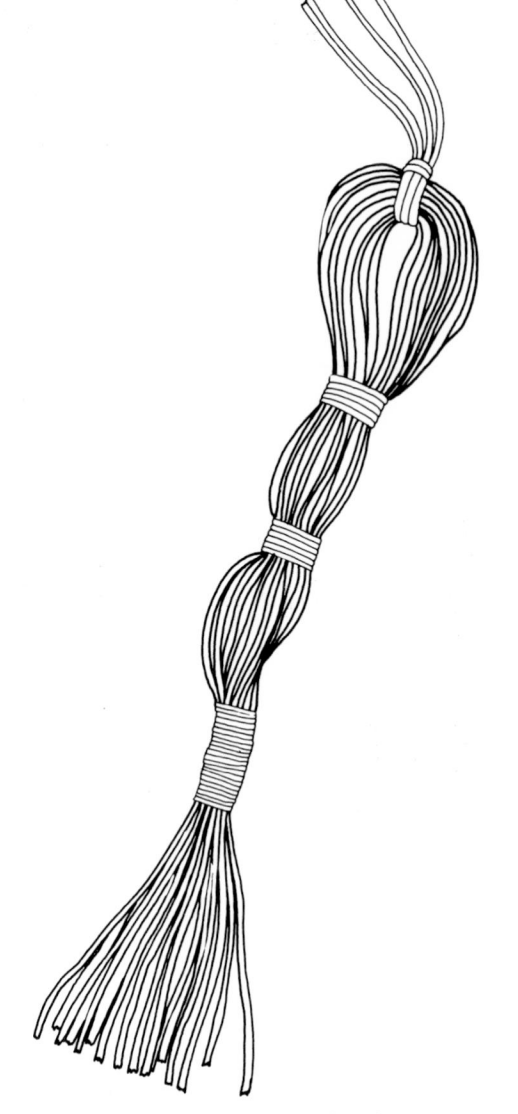

30 *Space-dyed threads: bind a skein or selection of threads at even or random intervals*

blue, turquoise or grey cold-water dye **(4)**. Leave your tied-up sample in the dyebath for only about ten minutes. It is worthwhile checking the depth of colour by taking the sample out of the dyebath and inspecting it after a few minutes. It can always be retied and immersed again. If you require a two- or three-colour effect, rinse and dry the fabric between each immersion. However, should

31 *Close-up of a pulled work panel on acrylic furnishing fabric. Space-dyed strips of chiffon are used for the eyelets*

you wish the colours to merge with each other, redye the wet sample straightaway. Always use the palest colour first. Pale blue or grey fabric can also be used, perhaps with the addition of a pale lilac dye. For sunsets use shades of orange, pink and yellow and for stormy skies grey, purple and navy.

For *vegetation* the process is similar, but use darker, more vibrant colours, such as shades of yellow, blue and dark green. Corduroy, towelling and cotton or panne velvet make very lush backgrounds and take hot- and cold-water dyes well.

To obtain an *underwater effect* the fabric can be crumpled lengthways so that darker areas will result at the bottom of the sample. A pale blue or pale green fabric can be dyed a variety of darker blues and greens. Cotton voile, organdie, nylon and other sheer materials give interesting watery effects. These could be overlaid on other fabrics dyed in similar or toning colours. For added lustre the under fabric could be acetate satin which takes the colour very well in hot-water dye. However if you require a pale colour, use a light shade and only dip for a minute or two.

Folded methods, bound or clamped

These are useful for *geometric and repeat designs* or motifs on practical articles includ-

1 *Close-up of a canvaswork footstool by the author; the design is based on a rock garden. Tie-dyed leaves and batik flowers are combined* *with a large variety of textured wools used for conventional canvaswork stitches and for improvised loops and knots*

2 'Pearl-bordered Fritillary' by the author: the painted wings are embroidered and stand out in relief. The quilted background illustrates another use for tie-dyed marbled fabric. (Courtesy of Mr and Mrs T. E. Knibb)

3 'Virginia Creeper' by the author: a painted batik background with tjanting lines outlining the brickwork, which has been subsequently quilted. The silk leaves are padded and some have piped edges. (Courtesy of Mr and Mrs G. Franklin)

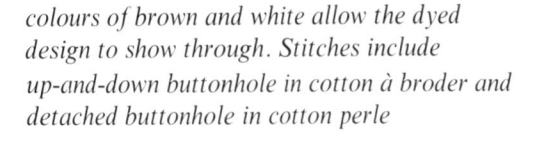

32 *Tie-dyed cushion design: the central light circle was made by tying up a large button, the remainder was folded and clamped with bulldog clips. Openwork embroidery in self colours of brown and white allow the dyed design to show through. Stitches include up-and-down buttonhole in cotton à broder and detached buttonhole in cotton perle*

ing cushions and curtains or on small items such as bags and place-mats (32). For the majority of articles of this type, to avoid wasting fabric, it is best to cut out the pattern pieces first to assess where the design should be, before dyeing. A geometric design for a square cushion can be made by folding the fabric in any of the square methods (see page 28). It may be necessary to refold and redye the opposite half or corner, if you require a symmetrical pattern. Rectangular designs can be folded by the rectangular method (see page 26) and clamped or bound in the method of your choice. Experiment with a range of regular and irregular stripes, either on the straight or diagonal, and chevrons. If the back of the cushion and any trimmings are to be in plain matching fabric, it is quickest and easiest to dye these at the same time. Satin acetate and nylon ribbon and cotton tape all dye very well and although each trim will emerge from the dyebath a slightly different colour, nevertheless it will tone very well with the background fabric. Cushions can be in satin, silk, linen, cotton velvet or calico.

Dowels and sticks

If the method employing dowels described on page 30 is used as follows, it will give a *fern-like effect*, which can have a number of decorative applications, particularly for landscapes with areas of vegetation. Fold a rectangle of fabric in three lengthways and then in half again also lengthways, so that the central area of the fabric is outermost (10a). Wind this strip diagonally round the dowel and bind it with fine yarn straight across (16). Dye in the colour of your choice. The fine tracery of chevrons which appears can also be cut up into leaves with ready imprinted veins (17) or used on an appliquéd or quilted picture of feather or fish images (33). For a more random result, gather the fabric up lengthways into a long bundle and wind this round a piece of dowel, securing with string or rubber bands. If the same process is used with

tape or ribbon, these will emerge from the dyebath with a wavy diagonal stripe. This can be used as a trimming or if appliquéd in adjacent lines, it gives a flowing, watery effect. For a diagonal pattern reminiscent of underwater plant-life, wind a single wide strip of fabric round an old rolling pin or a piece of plastic guttering and bind with a variety of different threads (34). This would look effective for an embroidered panel with stitchery in, for example, feather stitch to accentuate the frond shapes. Padded areas representing stones on the river bed could be added in leather or suede, possibly also tie-dyed.

Hardboard shapes

Quite large pieces of fabric suitable for garments such as jackets and waistcoats can be dyed by sandwiching the fabric between two pieces of shaped hardboard (36). This will produce a *rectangular but random design*, which lends itself either to English or Italian quilting. Fold the fabric, making sure that those areas you wish to be most prominent in colour and design are towards the outside. Select a pair of irregularly shaped pieces of hardboard slightly smaller than the folded sample and sandwich the sample between them. If you decide to fasten it with string or yarn, distribute the excess folds evenly either side of the hardboard. The bindings will leave a series of vein-like impressions between the irregular shapes of the hardboard. Alternatively the sample can be clamped with bulldog clips to hold the hardboard in place. For a uniformly coloured pattern, it may be necessary to refold part way through the dyeing process. This method can also be used to spark off new ideas, as very unusual designs will emerge, particularly if you look at the fabric through a window mount (3a,b).

With practice, designs for landscapes or trees and plants can be effected. These can be embroidered with hand or machine stitching, beads or quilting.

A combination of this hardboard method

33 *Quilted fish panel by the author: pure silk was twice dyed by the chevron method, folding and tying in the opposite direction the second time. The resultant fish images are* *trapunto quilted with a couched outline to emphasize the shapes; feather and buttonhole stitches are introduced to represent plant life*

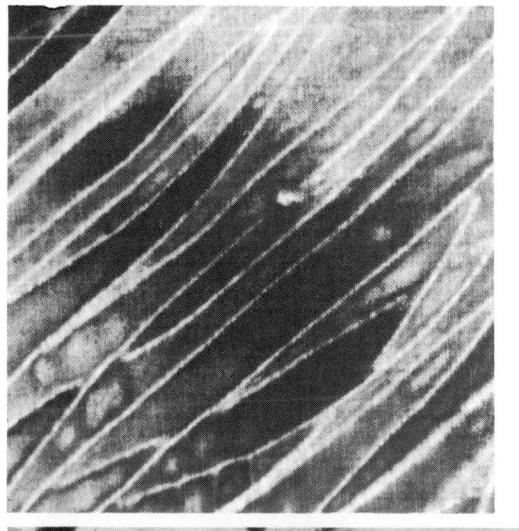

34 *Another example of tie-dye which could be used as in figure 33 for the background of an underwater panel. Fabric was rolled round a piece of plastic gutter and bound with a selection of threads*

36 Opposite *Green cotton quilted waistcoat by the author tie-dyed by the hardboard method; the fabric was carefully folded to ensure that the pattern on the front and the back of the garment bore a mirror image. The design for the lines of Italian quilting was suggested by the pattern of the tie-dye*

35 *This combination of marbling and hardboard methods* (37) *suggests a tree design suitable for enhancement with embroidery*

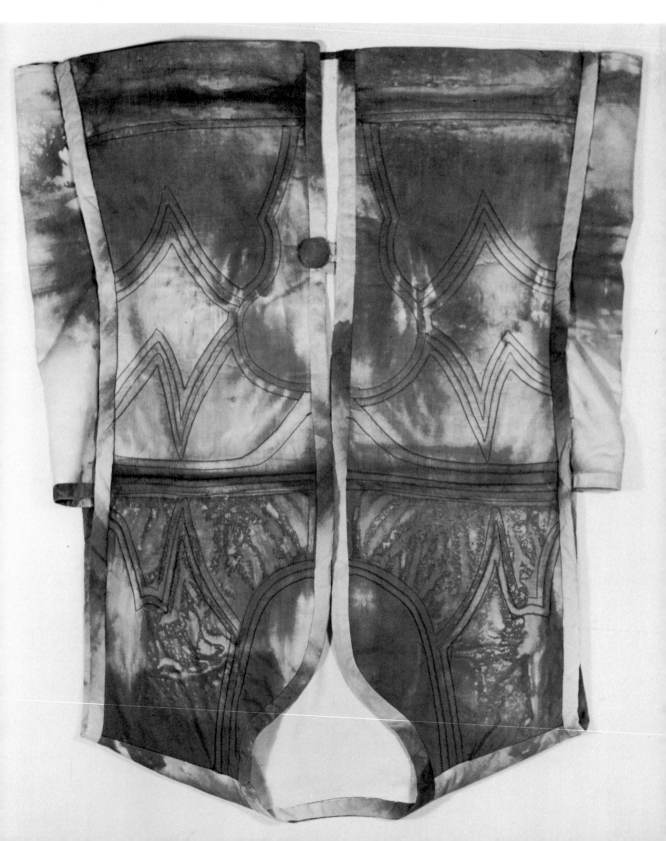

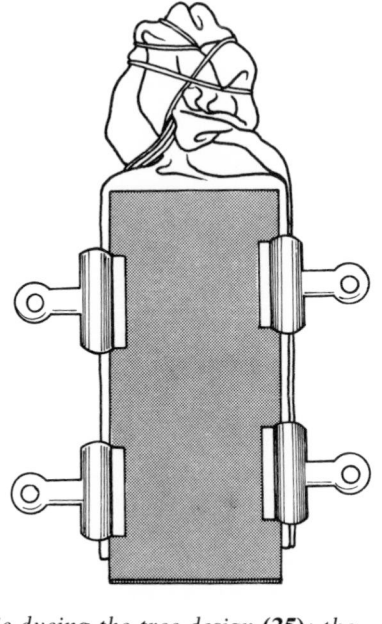

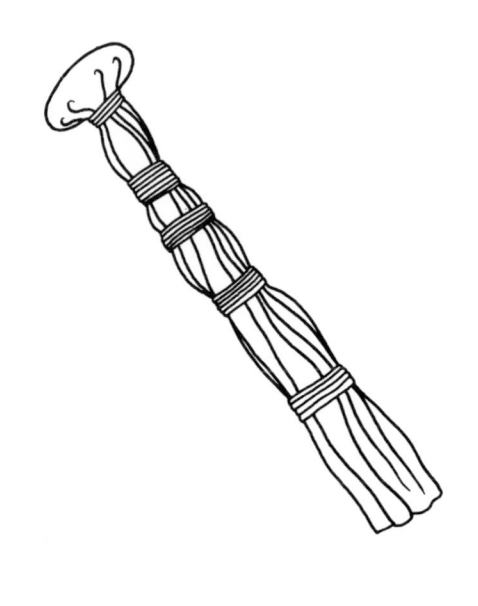

37 *Tie-dyeing the tree design* (35); *the foliage is marbled, the tree trunks clamped between two pieces of wood*

with marbling produces a design which evokes *a line of trees* (35). The trunks are formed by the lower half of the fabric being folded and clamped between two laths of wood. For the foliage the remainder of the fabric is marbled (37). Embroider with textured stitches such as French and bullion knots to accentuate the foliage and use open and closed chain for the tree trunks. Alternatively, additional trees or plants in stitchery or in relief can be introduced in the foreground.

Using objects

From your initial experiments you will realize that most objects such as pebbles, stones, buttons etc. produce sunburst or flowerlike images.

A single *sunburst design* is made with a large stone or button secured with rubber bands or string in the centre of a square of single fabric. The remainder of the bundle is then bound with more rubber bands at intervals, or with different thicknesses of string, tape or cotton

38 *Single sunburst design method: place a stone or button in the centre of the fabric and bind the remainder at intervals with string or rubber bands*

to give concentric circles (38,39). Dye a second time with the bindings moved to a different area. If you use bright colours and a fabric such as satin, a very vibrant design will appear. This could be enhanced with hand or machine embroidery. Another idea would be to dye at the same time a piece of transparent fabric with similar bindings. This could be superimposed a little to the side of the sunburst on the satin to give a double image.

Individual flowers are made by proceeding as for the sunburst, but usually on a smaller scale (41). Mark the position of each flower on the fabric before tying in the objects. Stalks can be made with precise folding of the fabric below each flower-head, each stalk being clamped between laths (40).

For an *overall background* of small flower shapes, cover the entire fabric with a variety of tied up buttons, beads, small stones, etc. (42). You will find innumerable uses for pieces such as this. They can either be used as back-

39 *Sunburst design, the result of tie-dyeing as in figure 38. This example was first dyed* *yellow; the bindings were then moved to other areas and it was dyed green*

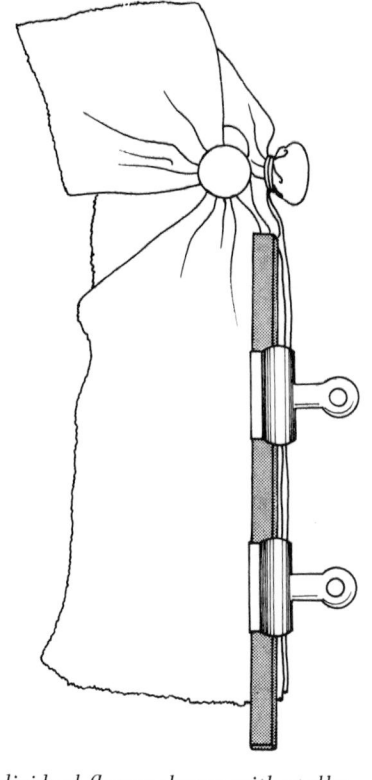

42 *Flower dots: similar buttons tied up in rows produce this flower-head pattern which could be used as part of an appliqué panel with each centre filled with stitchery. Alternatively each motif could be cut out and used separately*

41 *Individual flower shapes with stalks. Buttons are used for the central circular areas, and the stalks are clamped between laths of wood*

40 Opposite *Three flowers made as in figure 41, dyed first in orange and then in brown*

grounds for decorative panels or for cutting up for appliqué. If the buttons are spaced out a little, the fabric can be cut out and used for clamshell, petal or Suffolk puff patchwork. Another choice might be to use the flower-shaped pieces as trimmings on a garment either appliquéd or as a bias strip, or for covered buttons.

Rolling over a cord

The *mottled effect* produced by rolling the fabric over a cord is very useful to the embroiderer. It gives beautiful dappled effects suitable for all types of background and some

results so resemble reptile skin that they can be actually used unaltered for appliqué in a design of snakes, lizards etc. **(23)**. For this effect it is essential to use a very fine fabric such as cotton lawn or silk. Roll and bunch the fabric very tightly, without additional bindings and dye in either hot- or cold-water dyes.

Try a dappled background for an embroidered panel of a woodland scene with light filtering through the trees. For this, start with a gold or yellow material and dye it in dark blue or dark green. If the fabric is used singly and only rolled one way, it will be darker at one edge and gradually lessen in pattern and colour towards the top, giving a sense of depth to the piece. This could also be used reversed with the lighter area towards the bottom.

53

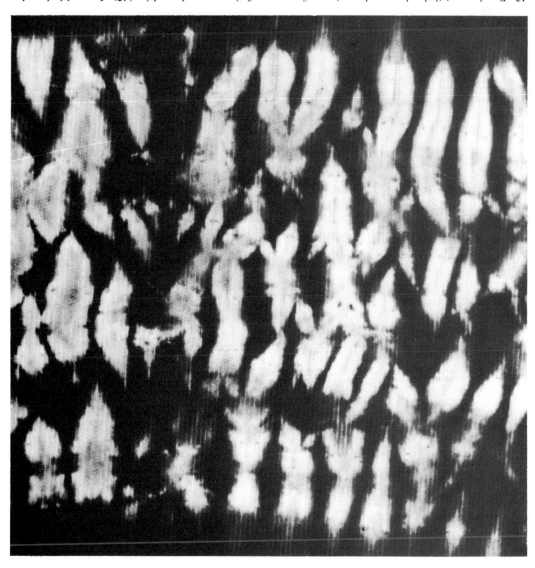

Tritik

It is possible with tritik to achieve quite specific designs. A very good random back-ground can be made quickly with one of the gathering methods. This has applications similar to those of the mottled effect described above, but the pattern tends to be reminiscent of tiger or zebra skin (43). It could thus be used in a child's bedroom for an appliquéd design of animals on the curtains or quilt, or would look well for an embroidered picture of a circus, zoo or jungle. For this effect, start at the top of the sample and gather with uneven length stitches across to the right; continue back to the left-hand side about 2.5 cm (1 in.) below the first row of stitching. Repeat this until the entire fabric is covered with lines of irregular stitches. Pull the thread tightly and

43 *Random tritik background: a piece of yellow corduroy dyed dark brown for use as part of an appliqué picture featuring a tiger*

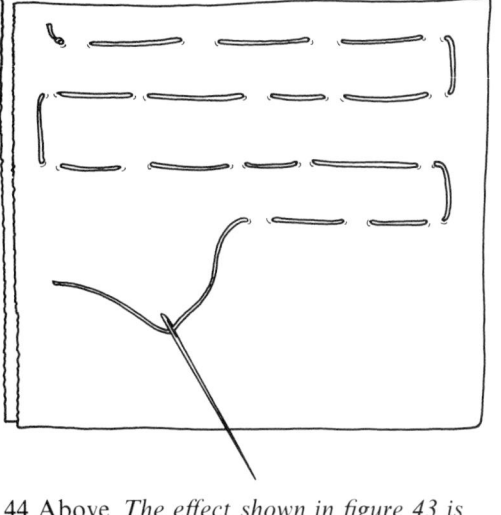

fasten off. This method can be used on single or folded fabric (44).

Tritik can also be used very simply for items such as decoratively striped cushions in calico, satin cotton or velvet. Gather, tuck and oversew across the width of the fabric in lines or concentric circles (26), leaving 6–8 cm (2–3 in.) between each row. Tape or ribbon dyed to match or contrast can be stitched

45 *'Peppers' by Morna Grafton: two of a set of four tritik panels in shades of grey, green and yellow. The main outlines were gathered before dyeing. The example on the right has couched twisted cords, beads and French knots; that on the left incorporates small appliqué shapes, with gold and soft embroidery thread and tiny sequins completing the effect*

44 Above *The effect shown in figure 43 is produced by random gathers on folded fabric tightly drawn up*

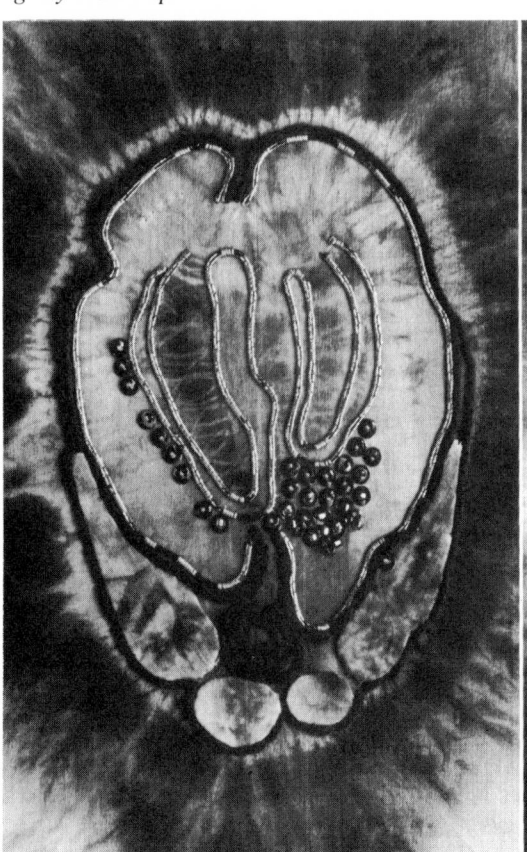

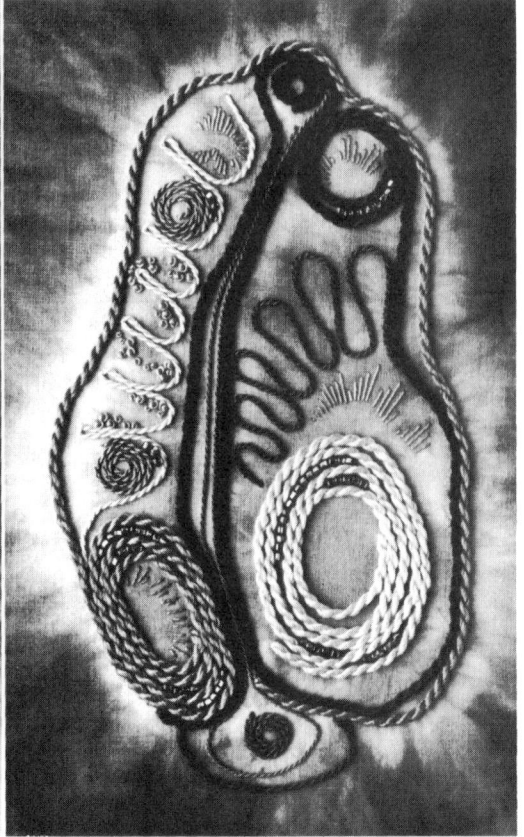

between the lines of tritik pattern. This method could also be used for borders on skirts and jackets. Accessories such as belts, cummerbunds and bags can have tritik designs, either as a major part of the design or as a small area of appliqué. Running stitches in zig-zag formation make beautiful borders or areas of pattern which lend themselves to being ornamented with stitchery or quilting.

Tritik can also be used for *outlining* a design or motif. This gives a negative image when dyed. A whole design for a tea-cosy or quilt can be stitched on the sewing machine in zig-zag stitch on either single or folded fabric. If your machine has an embroidery foot with a hole through it, thread this with a gimp and zig-zag over. This thread can then be pulled up tightly to gather the design for greater resist. After dyeing, unpick the stitches with a stitch-ripper or cut with small, sharp scissors. The resultant design can then be restitched alongside the undyed outline for either English or Italian quilting. This idea can also be worked with hand stitchery. Outline the design with a double or treble line of tiny running stitches and draw them up very tightly before fastening off securely and immersing in the dye **(27a)**.

A combination of tritik dots and outlines can be used for both abstract and realistic ideas. A quilted and embroidered panel in tritik-dyed fabric could be designed with animal forms, with leopards, utilizing the dots, and zebras, making use of either over-sewn or gathered lines.

Ombré and part-dyed fabrics

Shaded and part-dyed fabrics can be used in a variety of ways. Garments shading from dark to light from hem to waist are very attractive, as are quilted waistcoats with intricate designs in embroidery. For these it is obviously necessary to select a fabric which will not only dye well but will also be suitable for the particular garment. Silk chiffon or georgette is beautiful for scarves and for very full shaded dresses or overblouses, perhaps with the addition of beading or embroidery in silk threads. Cotton voile also dyes well. On pictures or embroidered panels the ombré method can be used for practically anything: for skies or backgrounds of landscapes, for areas of interest in abstract designs, or for more definite shaded effects for appliquéd pieces. Do not discard experimental ombré pieces which have not dyed evenly, or which have resulted in defined lines of colour across the sample. These can be looked at again through a window template **(3a,b)** and can be used as a background, or the fabric made into shapes for appliqué or patchwork. Part-dyed pieces and two-colour shaded pieces which have a central area in a third colour can also be reassessed in this way and successfully utilized. For areas of texture, fine and sheer fabrics also lend themselves very well to being draped, pleated or ruched before being stitched to the background.

4 BATIK

Batik, like tie-dye, is a resist process. In this case wax is used as the agent to prevent the dye penetrating the fabric. Several applications of wax in different parts of the design, alternated with dyeing, can gradually build up extremely intricate and colourful patterns or pictures. One of its most distinctive characteristics is the 'crackle' – the irregular network of fine lines which is produced by the dye infiltrating small cracks in the wax. Only natural fibres such as silk, cotton and linen are suitable as hot wax will have a detrimental effect on other fabrics. Only cold-water dyes may be used as hot-water dyes would cause the wax to melt.

Equipment for waxing

The working area should be covered with several layers of newspaper with waxed kitchen paper on top. Arrange your work space so that the heat source is immediately adjacent to the waxing area.

Electric hot-plate or cooker. This should be thermostatically controlled. It is not advisable to heat wax over the naked flame of a gas-cooker.

A heat-resistant mat. Place this alongside your heat source, and set your wax-pot on it as soon as the wax starts to smoke.

A wax-pot. This can be a double saucepan with water in the bottom and wax in the top, or a metal container in a saucepan of water. (The wax can be heated in a heavy saucepan, but extreme care should be taken that it does not get too hot.)

Brushes. Various sizes will be needed, from decorator's brushes to fine artist's brushes. It is advisable to buy fairly cheap brushes and replace them frequently, as they deteriorate quite rapidly in use with wax. Some brushes can be cut to various shapes to give different types of line, or double and treble lines **(47)**.

A tjanting. This is a small tool, traditionally used to produce dots and fine lines **(47)**. It has a small reservoir, usually in brass or copper, for holding the wax and a very fine spout through which the wax flows. Although not necessary for preliminary experiments, it is a useful additional tool, as the effect it produces cannot be achieved in any other way.

A batik frame. This can be an artist's stretcher frame, an old picture frame, or a home-made one constructed from four pieces of wood nailed into a rectangular shape. For very small designs a circular wooden embroidery frame would suffice.

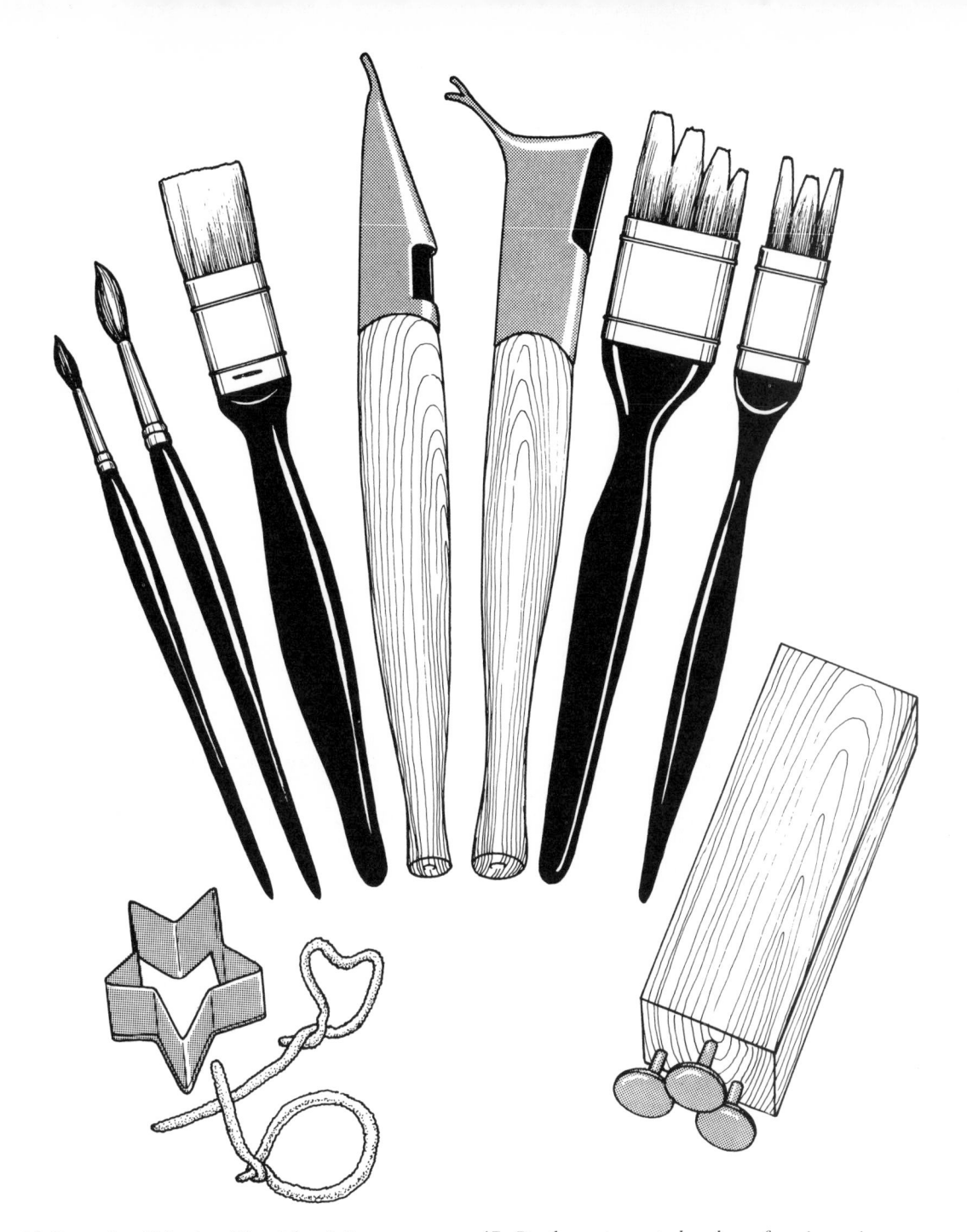

46 Opposite 'Market Place' by Julia Beevers; the 'crackle' effect on this subtle olive green and fawn batik is highlighted with free machine embroidery suggesting an early morning or twilight atmosphere. The two principal figures are trapunto quilted

47 Batik equipment: brushes of various sizes, including those cut for producing multiple lines; single and double-spouted tjantings; tjaps made from a pastry cutter, pipe-cleaners and tacks mounted on wood

Tjaps. These are printing blocks, rather like metal biscuit or pastry cutters, used in Indonesia, and made of an intricate latticework of metal sheets and rods, which, when dipped in hot wax and pressed hard onto the cloth, imprint a pattern. Home-made tjaps can be fashioned out of a variety of different objects –

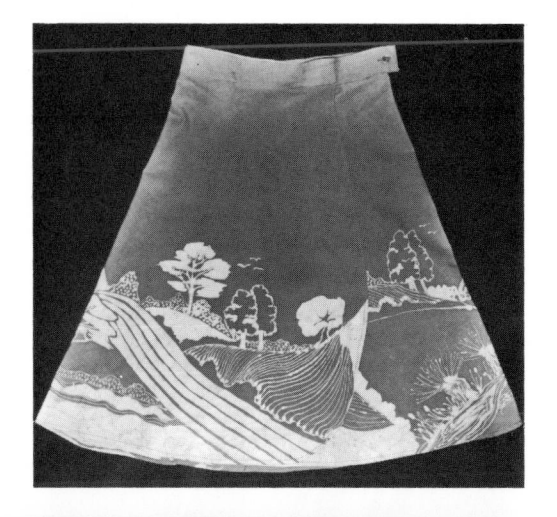

48 *(a) Cotton batik skirt by Sian Kibblewhite. This incorporates the use of the tjanting for the fine lines and dots, and also brushwork for the more solid areas (b) Detail of the skirt*

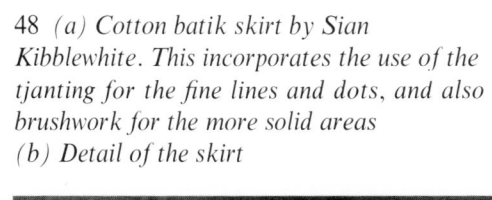

blocks of wood, cardboard stuck onto wood, or corks cut into interesting shapes. Metal objects such as pastry cutters or nails should be attached to a wooden handle. Pipe-cleaners can be bent to form circular shapes, loops, stars or flowers.

Wax. Various waxes are suitable for batik. For the beginner it is probably easiest to purchase a ready prepared batik wax – this is a combination of paraffin wax and beeswax. If you wish to make your own mixture, the most satisfactory proportions are one-third beeswax and two-thirds paraffin wax. Beeswax is expensive and very malleable, so it is not suitable for use alone. Paraffin wax is brittle and will crack very readily. Microcrystalline wax has similar properties to beeswax.

Equipment for dyeing

Cover the working surfaces with plastic or newspaper and wear rubber gloves and protective clothing.

A plastic or enamel container. Two types are needed – a bucket large enough to hold sufficient water in which to submerge the fabric completely, and also a shallow vessel for those designs in which you do not wish the wax to crack.

A measuring jug and bowl.

Plastic spoons. For measuring and stirring.

A kettle.

Fabrics

The same preliminary rules apply as for tie-dye (page 21), but only natural fibres such as silk, cotton and linen are suitable. Use finely woven, non-stretch, smooth-surface fabrics for best results. New fabrics should be washed, dried and ironed to remove any dressing.

49 Indigo-dyed tjap designs from Bali. In the left-hand example the tjap has been lightly stamped and the central white area painted with wax; the right-hand design uses the same tjap with more wax applied to produce a thicker imprint and it is linked with an additional tjap motif

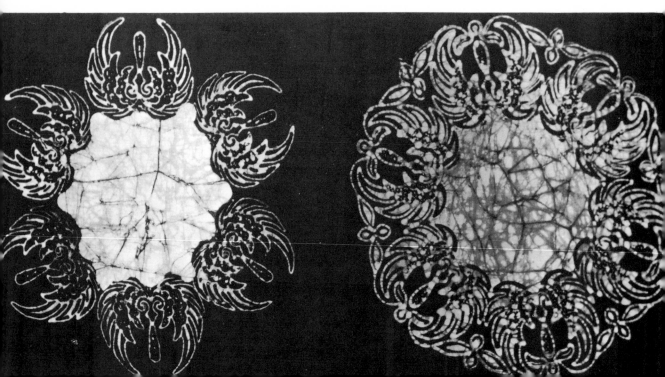

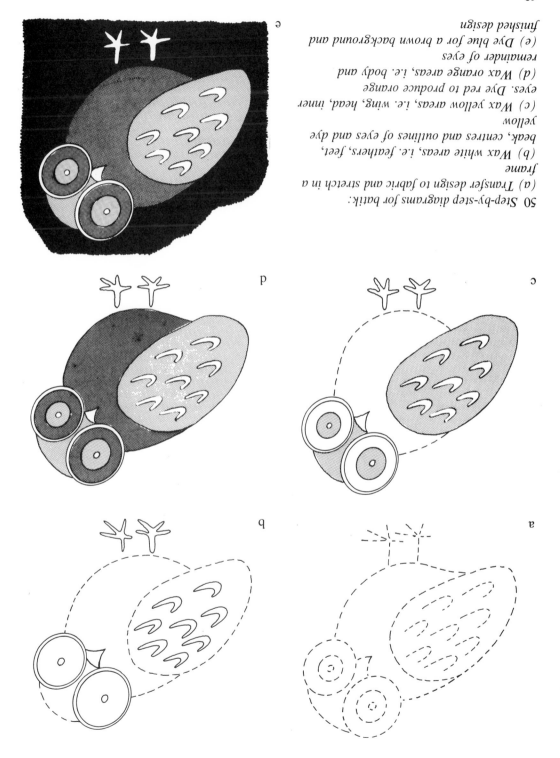

50 Step-by-step diagrams for batik:
(a) Transfer design to fabric and stretch in a frame
(b) Wax white areas, i.e. feathers, feet, beak, centres and outlines of eyes and dye yellow
(c) Wax yellow areas, i.e. wing, head, inner eyes. Dye red to produce orange
(d) Wax orange areas, i.e. body and remainder of eyes
(e) Dye blue for a brown background and finished design

Dyes

Use cold-water dyes only (see pages 21–2).

General method for batik

Before beginning, it is important to understand the basic principle of building up a design in batik **(50)**. The wax will act as a resist to the first dyebath, so the first application of wax needs to cover those areas which you wish to remain white (or the colour of the original fabric). The first dyebath should contain the palest colour, e.g. yellow. The second waxing will be on those areas which you wish to remain yellow. The second dye should be the next darkest colour and will combine with the first in those areas left unwaxed, so that if the first dye is yellow and the second red, then orange will result. Next, those areas required to be orange should be waxed and the final dyeing in, for example, blue will result in a brown.

Transferring the design

Only the main lines of the design need to be transferred to the fabric. This can be done by one of the following methods.

Freehand, directly on to the fabric, using charcoal, a soft pencil or a water-erasable marker (sold for use in quilting).

Using a light-box. If one is not available, attach the design firmly to a window-pane (in daylight). Secure the fabric on top so that the light shines through and trace the design.

Tracing direct. This can be done if the fabric is fine enough for the design to show through.

For a repeat design, cut a *template* of the main outline and draw round it.

Pricking and pouncing is a traditional method useful for intricate or repeat designs. Trace the design on either greaseproof or tracing paper. Turn the design over and pin it face down on a soft surface such as a piece of blanket or several layers of felt. With a darning needle prick along the traced lines, at short intervals. Position and pin the tracing with the right side uppermost on to the fabric. Make a small roll of doubled felt about 2–3 cm (1 in.) in diameter and bind it with a piece of yarn. Dip this into a mixture of powdered chalk and charcoal and with a circular movement, rub it over the design, forcing the powder through the holes. Carefully remove the tracing paper and the design will be revealed in small dots on your fabric. The design can then easily be drawn in with a soft pencil or water-erasable pen. For a repeat pattern, re-use the same tracing.

Preparation of fabric

Having transferred the design to the fabric, stretch it over your chosen frame with drawing pins or staples, keeping the grain straight and the fabric taut.

Method

Waxing

In a double saucepan or wax-pot, slowly melt the chosen wax. Do not fill the pan more than half full. The wax is ready when slightly smoking – if you are using a thermostatically controlled hot-plate you will be able to regulate the heat. Should the wax start to give off thick smoke, remove the pan immediately from the heat, place on a heat-resistant mat and allow to cool a little. *Never* allow the wax to be left on the heat unattended.

Waxing with brush or tjanting
Have ready either the lid of a jar or a small flat pad of folded newspaper covered with a piece of rag, to use as a drip-pad when you are

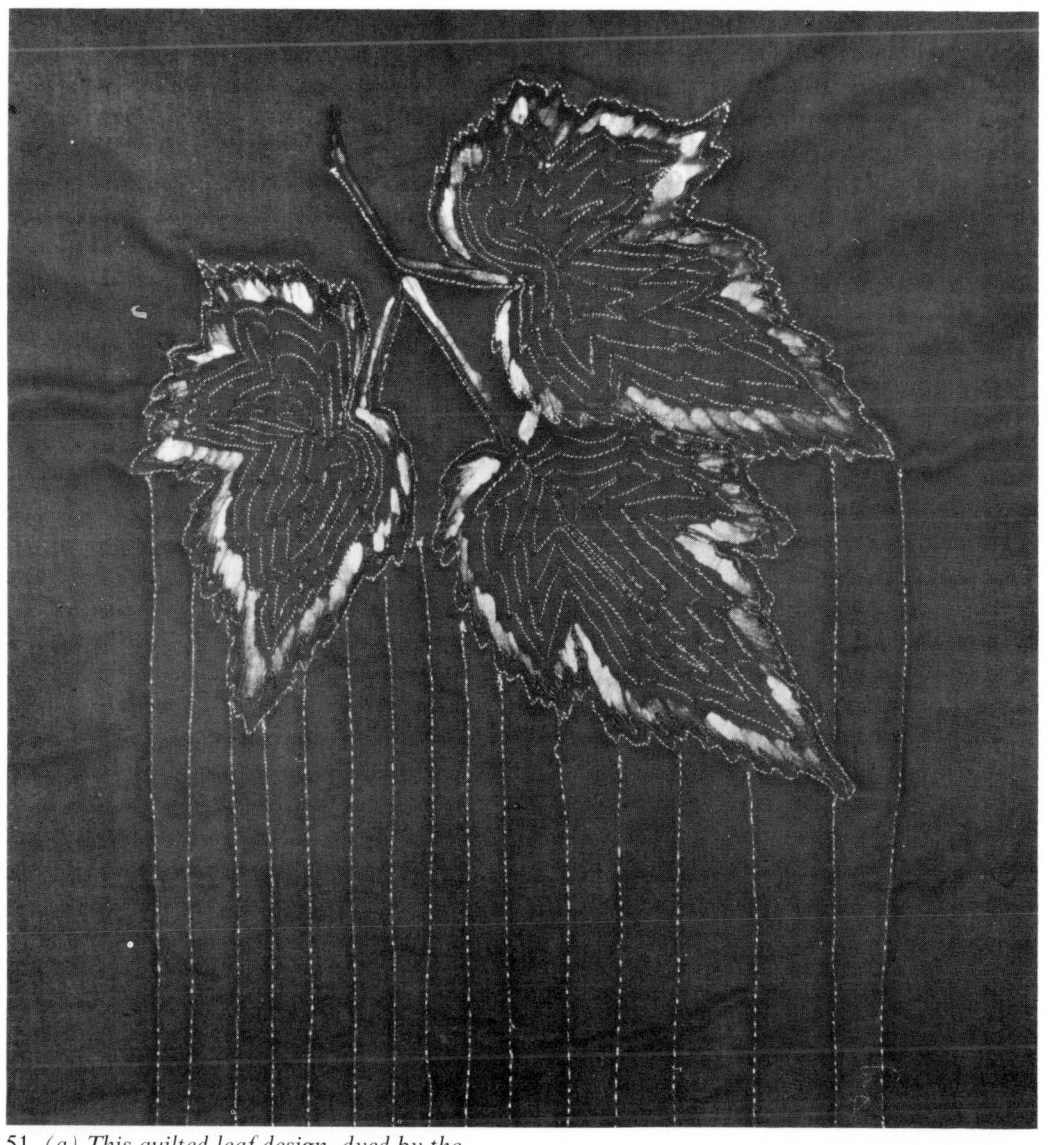

51 *(a) This quilted leaf design, dyed by the author and machine embroidered by Naomi Cohen-Ziv, was achieved by brushing hot wax over the edge of an actual leaf pinned to the fabric*

transferring the brush or tjanting from the wax-pot to your design. Dip the brush or tjanting into the wax and hold it there for 10–15 seconds to heat up. The reservoir of the tjanting should not be too full or the wax will flow over the top as well as through the spout with disastrous results!

Try out the temperature of the wax on a spare piece of fabric – the wax should have a transparent appearance when it touches the fabric, which means it has fully penetrated the fibres. If it is opaque, then the wax is not hot enough, and it will not resist the dye. If it is too

(b) batik outline prior to being embroidered

(c) Suggestion for use of the above motif

hot, it will flow too rapidly through the spout of the tjanting or from the bristles of the brush and spread. It is particularly important when using the tjanting for fine lines to make sure you get it right the first time, as it is impossible to retrace exactly the same line. However, larger areas, which have been brushed, can be rewaxed satisfactorily on both the back and front of the work. Hold the fabric up to the daylight from time to time to ensure that the wax has penetrated thoroughly. Remember that the wax cools down very rapidly, so you need to work quickly and refill the brush or tjanting frequently. When the first waxing is complete, prepare the cold-water dye (see page 21), wet the fabric thoroughly in cold water and carefully immerse in the dyebath. When dyeing is completed, dry thoroughly

before rewaxing. Proceed with subsequent waxings and dyeings until you have achieved the result you require.

'Crackle'

The fine network of veins particularly characteristic of batik will result if the waxed fabric is crumpled in the hand before immersing in the dye. The colour will seep through the cracks in the wax. The type of wax used will have some bearing on the quality of the crackle: for more crackle use a greater proportion of paraffin to beeswax; for less crackle use more beeswax or microcrystalline. For a fine crackle effect, it is helpful either to soak the waxed fabric in cold water or to place it in a freezer or refrigerator for ten minutes. This will make the wax more brittle and it can then be crushed either all

65

99

over or in those areas of the design where crackle is most needed. For a design with a stripe through it, simply crease the waxed fabric into folds where you wish the lines to

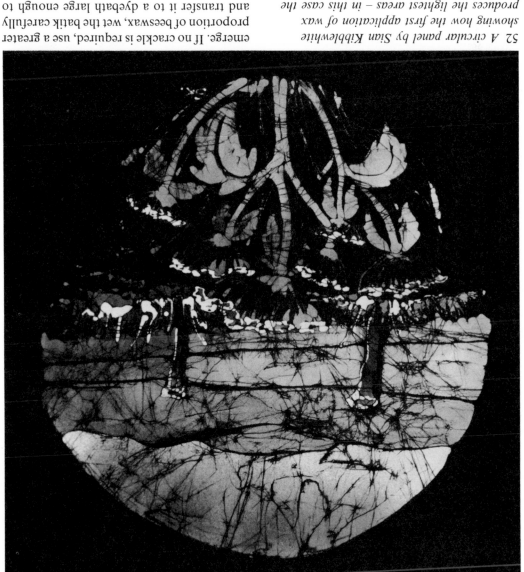

52 A circular panel by Sian Kibblewhite showing how the first application of wax produces the lightest areas – in this case the highlights on the fence posts and on the plant in the foreground. In addition, the sky was sprayed before the first waxing, giving a less stark contrast between land and sky.

emerge. If no crackle is required, use a greater proportion of beeswax, wet the batik carefully and transfer it to a dyebath large enough to accommodate the entire fabric without creasing.

Tjaps

For the batik stamping methods with a tjap, follow the same procedure as for the tjanting or brush. Dip the home-made tjap in the wax, shake off the excess and stamp the tjap hard on to the fabric. It is easier with this method to

tape the fabric to the working surface (covered with waxed kitchen paper) rather than have the work pinned to a frame. The same rules apply in that the wax must penetrate through to the back of the fabric. The fabric can then either be crumpled to achieve crackle or dyed flat in a shallow dyebath.

Removal of wax

On completion of the waxing and dyeing process it is necessary to remove the wax using an electric iron. Cover the ironing board with several layers of newspaper and a layer of kitchen paper towel. Put the batik on top of this and cover with another sheet of paper towel and one or two sheets of newspaper. Set the iron to the fabric setting for the particular fabric and iron off the wax through the paper. You will have to change both the top and bottom papers quite often. Continue until all

the wax has disappeared. The fabric will still be rather stiff and if you wish to soften it in order to embroider it, dip it in carbon tetrachloride (obtainable from the chemist's) in a well-ventilated room or out of doors, or better still take it to be drycleaned.

Experiments

Experiments in batik fall more or less into three groups. Firstly, a series of *random*

53 *'Farmhouse Window' by the author: a panel in the same series as figure 4, this time using the batik 'crackle' background to represent the tracery of winter trees. The tankards and plant pot are fabric-covered card; the cyclamen has silk-embroidered leaves and blooms*

only fabrics made of natural fibres, and cold-water dyes. Follow the general method for batik and the waxing process described on pages 63–6.

Batik with a tjanting

Dots

With heated wax in a tjanting, make an all-over random design of dots and dye the lightest colour. Repeat the process with more dots and dye the next darkest shade. This can be repeated as many times as you wish. For different shades of the same colour, a short dyeing period can be followed, after the next

designs can be made which can either be used as an interesting alternative to a plain back-ground fabric, or cut up for appliquéd pat-terns; secondly stamped designs can be made with a home-made tjap, which are useful for formal patterns or borders for household articles, children's and adults' clothes; lastly, and more usually, batik is used to create a realistic picture or design. Remember to use

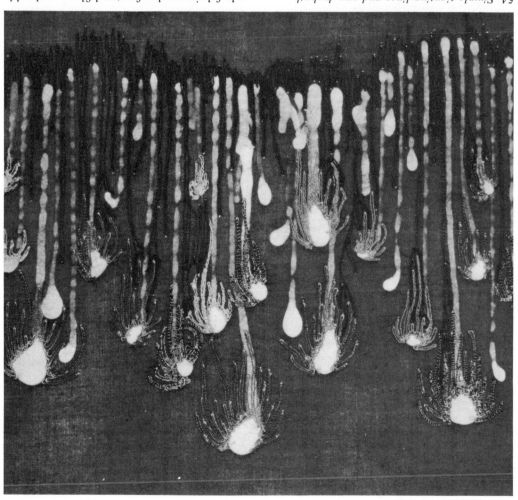

54 Simple tjanting lines and one dyebath produces this plant-form sample; the machine embroidery in whip stitch by Naomi Cohen-Ziv adds texture and additional form to the piece

4 'Palm Tree' by the author: the background of this small panel was dyed using the tie-dye hardboard method. Additional vertical tree trunks are couched space-dyed threads and the fronds of the palm are marbled cotton voile

5 'Clouds over Loch Earn' by Ann Green. The sky of this canvaswork panel has been left unworked and has been lightly painted. Conventional canvas stitches in a variety of threads fill the central area and the foreground stands out in relief with padded leather rocks embroidered with French knots

6 *Experimental panel by Fiona Hopcroft. The background has been sprayed, and bands of copper sheet sandwich together layers of similarly-coloured fabric which are frayed at either end. Added textural interest is introduced with couched metal threads.* (Courtesy of the Embroiderers' Guild)

7 *Machine- and hand-embroidered panel by Verina Warren on pure silk with silk bindings; the central areas have been sprayed and the decorative bands and other details painted.* (Photo: Stewart Warren. Courtesy of Mr and Mrs I. Joyce)

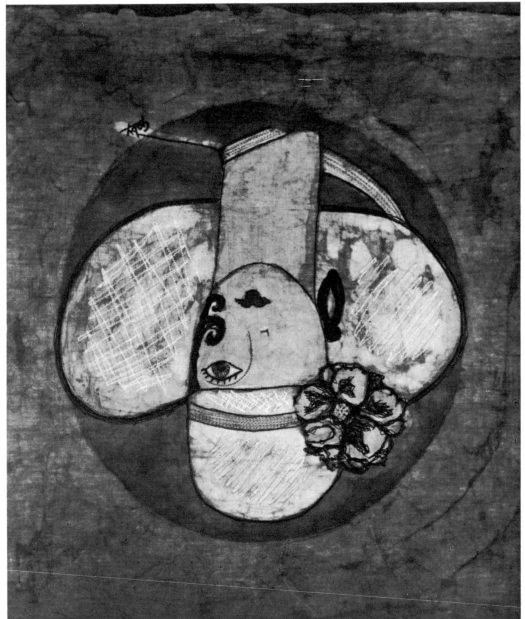

55 *'Woman in a White Hat'* by Gabriella Griso clearly shows the bold use of a brush and the various stages of waxing and dyeing: the hat was waxed first, to keep it white, and the first dyebath was fawn. Next the face, neck and flower were waxed and an orange dyebath used. The main background was waxed last, which left only the circular area to take the final brown dye. Machine stitchery outlines and reinforces some elements of the design and the eye and mouth are stitched by hand.

application of wax, with a longer period in the same dyebath. For a similar result, if you do not possess a tjanting, use a lighted household candle and drip the wax at random.

Lines

For a random pattern of irregular lines, follow the same procedure as for dots. The lines made with a tjanting always start with a small blob, so the type of design made should not be too rigid or precise. It is most suitable for flowing natural lines and good for plants, trees and flowers **(54)** and Art Nouveau-style designs. For geometric or very formal compositions, it is better to use a fine brush.

Brushed backgrounds

A 5 cm (2 in.) brush filled with wax covers large areas quickly and effectively **(55)** and of course produces an entirely different result from the tjanting. Use it very freely; do not try to be too precise. Experiment with undulating lines brushed across the fabric to produce a background for a seascape or flowing stream. On the same theme, a circular pattern could represent a whirlpool or tornado. All these could be embroidered with hand or machine stitches in textured threads. A combination of simple wide and narrow brushstrokes interspersed with tjanting dots could be used for a design depicting a waterfall, surf breaking, or indeed any sort of watery background. Lines of couching would strengthen the brush strokes and beads or French knots give added weight to the dots. A panel or wallhanging, inspired by Japanese or Chinese prints, could have the fabric decorated in this way.

Other ideas for embroidered pictures with more precise striped backgrounds could be those depicting the bars of, for example, a lion's cage or even those of a prison! For a more familiar subject, a trellis could be painted in wax and decorated with embroidered and appliquéd foliage.

56 *Simple repeat patterns can be quickly produced by waxing with a large brush cut to give multiple lines*

a

57 *(a) Brushed batik lines on a pair of child's dungarees make a background for an appliqué ship motif*

70

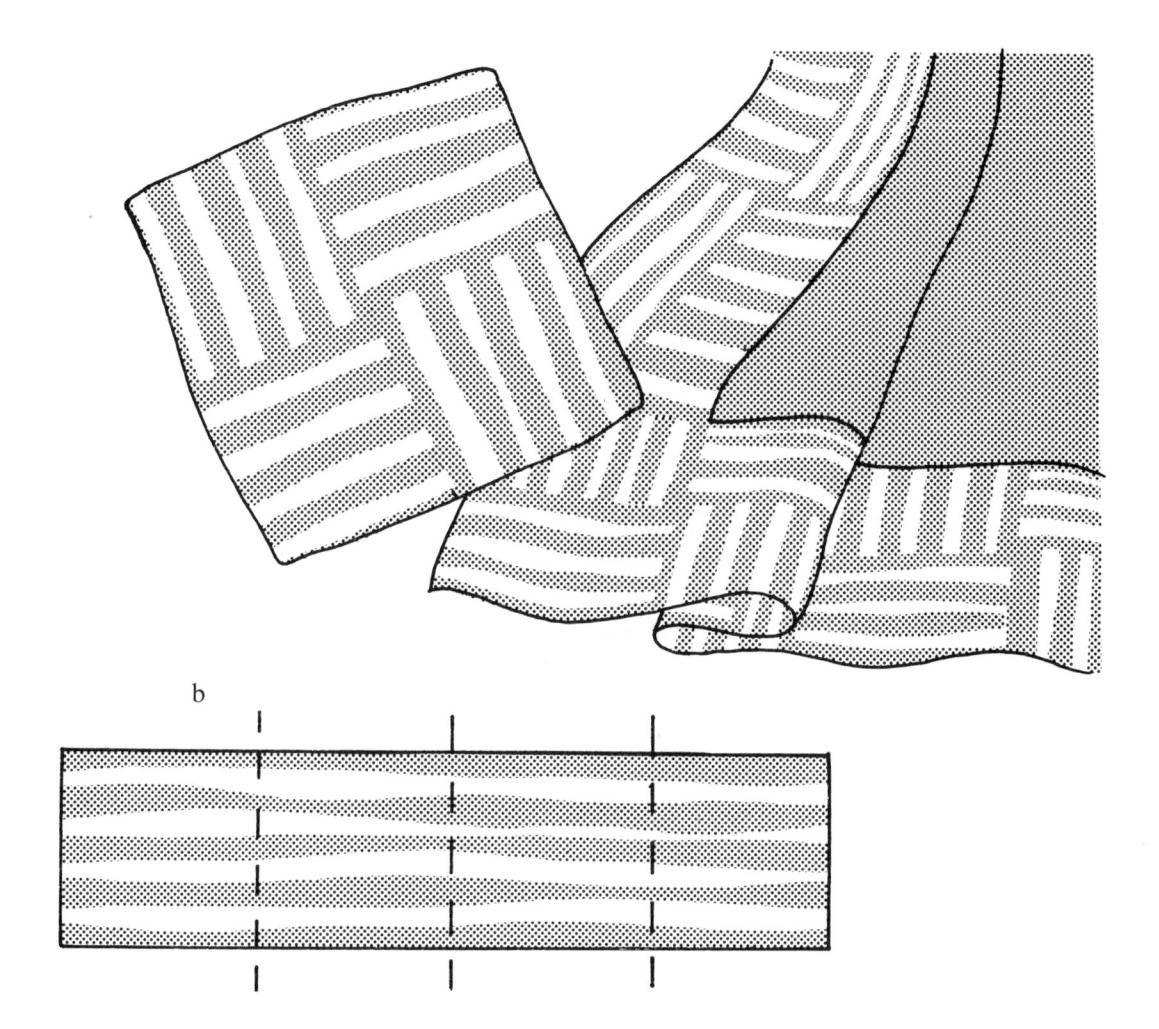

b

Brushes of different sizes, and those cut to give double and treble lines could make simple striped and geometric patterns **(56)**, which could afterwards be decorated very effectively with embroidery, perhaps with the application of ribbons and cords. Bands of stitches could accentuate a striped batik design: a pair of dungarees with a wide batik stripe could have a superimposed motif appliquéd on the stripe **(57a)**. Stripes can either be outlined in stitches such as couching or stem-stitch, or can themselves be embroidered with decorative details such as animals or flowers. Other geometric symbols such as triangles or circles

57 (b) A strip of fabric brushed with batik stripes can be cut up into squares and used for Seminole patchwork on cushions and curtains

could be applied to a design to break up the striped surface. As an alternative to appliqué or stitchery, the striped fabric could be cut up into large squares and realigned with the stripes at right-angles to each other, Seminole patchwork-fashion, to make a cushion or border to decorate curtains, bed-linen etc. **(57b)**. A brushed background using the 'crackle' effect looks very like the tracery of winter

71

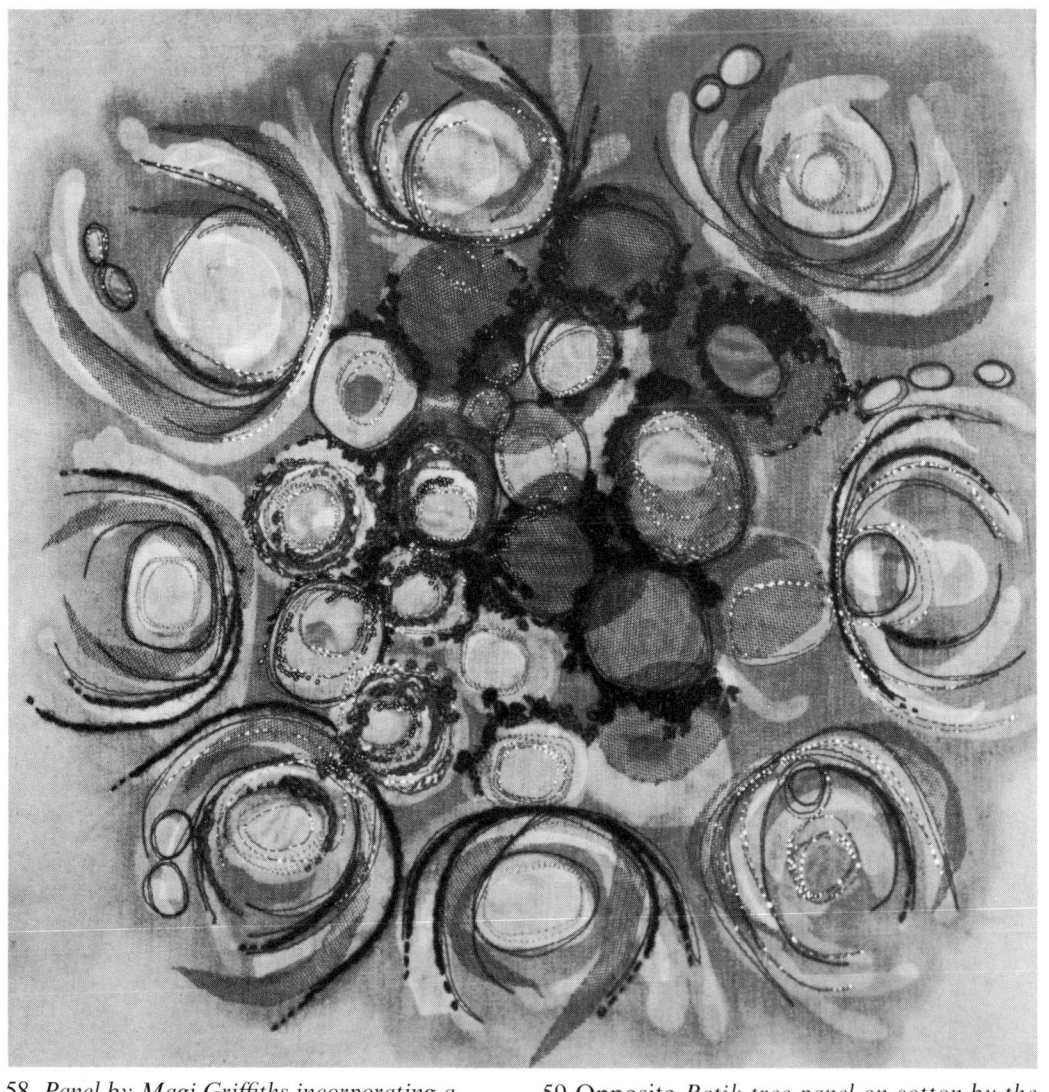

58 *Panel by Magi Griffiths incorporating a brushed batik design with circles of net and machine embroidery*

trees against the sky **(59)**. Start with a blue or grey background – this could also be shaded (see ombré method, page 41). Brush over the fabric with wax. When this is hard, crumple the fabric all over or in those areas where you require the crackle and dye dark green, brown or dark grey. Off-cuts of this fabric can also be used for appliquéd leaves with the crackle representing the veins **(4)**.

59 Opposite *Batik tree panel on cotton by the author. Only the top area was crackled to represent the tracery of branches. Stitchery in cotton perle and crochet cotton helps to darken some lighter tones and also to outline and add texture to the foreground* (Courtesy Mrs Jane Dunn)

Tjaps

Many decorative patterns, particularly repeat and all-over designs, can be made with tjaps of

cleaner tjaps bent into a flower or star shape can be added to a design for a picture of a garden or used as a border. A linen table cloth can have fruit or vegetable shapes stamped around the edge. For a co-ordinated bedroom scheme, add a batik tjap design to hems of sheets and pillowcases and use the off-cuts to decorate lampshades and curtains with ap-pliqué. Indeed, an all-over patterned fabric can be made with this method and can be used for an entire garment. This, of course, may not necessarily lend itself to further ornamen-tation with embroidery, though it may be possible to pick out some areas of the actual design or parts of the garment such as the yoke, collar or cuffs, which could be further embellished. The motifs in these areas could be filled with stitchery or outlined with a

different shapes and materials. The image will, of course, be reversed since the stamped motif will resist the dye and the background will be coloured (60). A motif can either be stamped apart from its neighbour or it can be over-lapped. Try different combinations of your selection of tjaps to make a number of designs. Experiment with all-over, repeat and half-drop patterns, borders, alternating and over-lapping images and random effects (61). The permutations are endless and the results can be used as you choose, either for incorporat-ing in decorative panels or wallhangings, or for enhancing your home or wardrobe. Pipe-

60 Linen table mat with applied motifs and some stitchery; the batik tjap pattern was made with a star-shaped pastry cutter

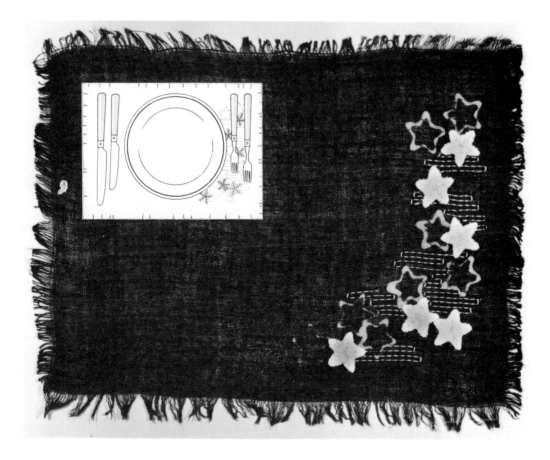

contrasting thread. For some designs, Italian quilting would give texture without introducing additional colour. A plain fabric dyed at the same time as the batik length could serve as a trimming, and this could be embroidered. For example, a dress in an all-over tjap pattern of stars and circles could have a plain collar and cuffs with these motifs embroidered or quilted, either in contrasting or toning thread.

A batik picture

Waxing and dyeing

Batik lends itself to many forms of design, both realistic and abstract. Ideas for inspiration can be found in natural and man-made forms. It is important to plan the various stages of waxing and dyeing before beginning and to remember that the technique necessitates starting with the palest colour and continuing with ever-darkening tones. Do not forget that they *combine* with each other, so if, on a white fabric, the first dye is yellow and the second blue, the two will combine to make green in the second dyebath. The finished batik will be white, yellow and green, with only a little blue, which may have seeped through any cracks in the wax covering the white background. If the original fabric is already a pale colour, the first dye will combine with that colour, i.e. a pale pink background dyed blue will produce mauve.

Having decided on the design, for example, a large flower-head, draw it out to the scale of the finished picture and mark in the appropriate colour where each dye will be (62). Follow one of the methods on page 63 for transferring the design and for the preparation of the fabric. Start by waxing, with a tjanting, the centre of the flowerhead with dots and small lines radiating from the centre. Dye in the palest colour, e.g. pink. The fabric will now be entirely pink except the areas which have been waxed. Dry thoroughly before beginning the second application of

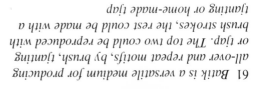

61 *Batik is a versatile medium for producing all-over and repeat motifs, by brush, tjanting or tjap. The top two could be reproduced with brush strokes, the rest could be made with a tjanting or home-made tjap*

62 (a) Draw design and decide on colour sequence

(b) Wax white areas with tjanting dots and lines for flower centre and dye pink

(c) Wax pink areas, i.e. inner parts of petals and dye blue to produce mauve

(d) Wax mauve areas, i.e. the remainder of the flower

(e) Dye background in green to produce brown

wax, this time brushing the inner areas of the petals. The second dyebath could be blue, which will produce mauve. Now apply the wax for the third time, covering the remainder of the petals which will stay mauve. The third dyebath will then be used for the background. Use a darker colour such as brown or dark green. These will combine with the mauve to give a shade of brown.

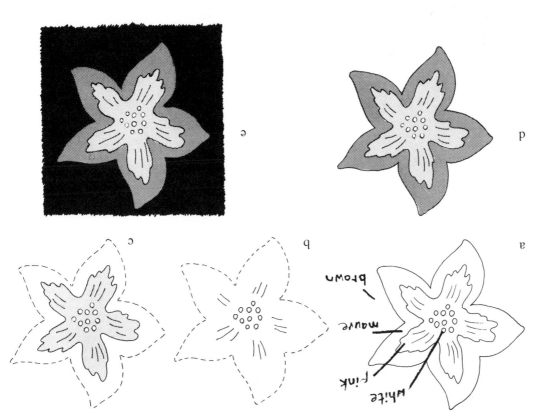

Unless you particularly wish the design to be defined with a white line, avoid the common mistake of outlining the entire picture with the first application of wax. Careful dyeing is essential to ensure that the surrounding plain areas dye evenly. Wet out the fabric thoroughly before immersing it in the dyebath and stir gently from time to time during the dyeing period. A way to eliminate the problem of having to worry about the background being dyed an even colour is to cover it with wax at the first waxing stage and 'crackle' it all

63 This batik picture by Sian Kibblewhite is inspired by a Japanese print and shows the use of a 'crackle' background, tjanting lines for the hair, and large brushed areas. This design is not in fact embroidered – there is already sufficient detail and pattern to make additional stitchery unnecessary

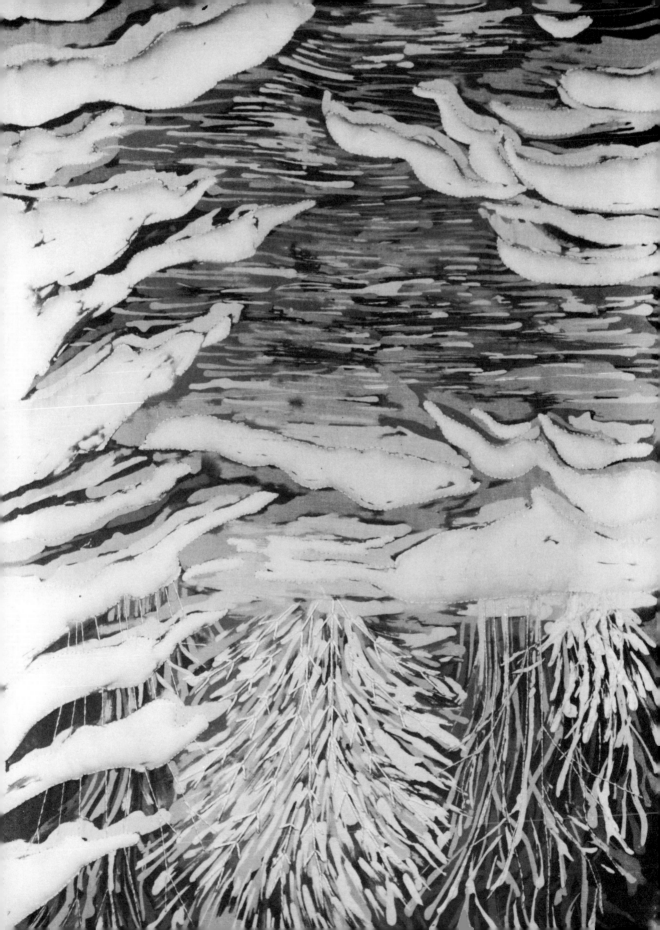

over, leaving out the third dyebath. This will give a white, pink and mauve flower with a crackled background in pink and mauve on white.

Embroidery

For a batik picture which is probably by its very nature quite intricately patterned, the balance between the subsequent embroidery and the dyed design must be carefully considered. To ornament an already complex picture might mean that you destroy the effect you have just created. However, one way of achieving a good result is the addition of texture to the flat surface. This could be with one of the types of quilting. Certain parts of

64 'Snow Scene' by Carol Leigh: brushed batik panel in two shades of blue creating a cold wintry scene; some areas are padded by Trapunto quilting. The vegetation in the background is reinforced with stitchery

65 'At the Seaside' by Gabriella Griso. Machine embroidery outlines and strengthens the deckchair forms and adds small areas of texture

the design could be padded or stuffed using trapunto quilting to emphasize the form **(64)**. Italian quilting could reinforce some of the linear aspects of a design, or the whole piece could be outlined either by hand or machine with English quilting. Any of these methods would be suitable for purely decorative use in a panel or wallhanging, or could have practical application for a cushion or quilt. When using batik, or indeed tie-dye, for a large item such as a quilt, it is best to plan the design so that it is made up in sections, as the practical difficulties of waxing and dyeing enormous lengths of fabric are great. However, it is perfectly possible to wax and dye smaller pieces of fabric and join them together later. If you wish the background colour to be the

same throughout, it will be necessary to dye all the pieces together, in which case you will have to transfer your dyeing activities to the bathroom! Trimmings, such as bindings, can be dyed at the same time.

Other sorts of texture can be applied to areas of batik. The centre of a flower or parts of a landscape can be decorated with beads or stitches. A delicate tracery of needleweaving in a fine thread can serve to reflect the network of crackle in other parts of the design. Stitches, such as the various chain stitches, stem stitch etc., can strengthen selected lines. Sometimes such stitches can help to restore some aspect of weakness, for example, by covering a wavy line to make it look straighter. An area which would look better in a lighter or darker tone could be improved with the addition of appropriately coloured stitches. Highlights can be added with outlines or areas of couching in metal threads, or pieces of gold or silver kid could be applied.

5 PAINTING, SPRAYING & DRAWING

Painting and drawing can be used to enhance your embroidery, either before starting the work, or to add highlights as it develops, or lastly as a finishing touch. Spraying is best completed before you begin to embroider as it is the most difficult technique to control successfully until you become proficient. However, good results can be achieved with the use of masking tape and stencils.

Painting and spraying

Equipment

Cover the working surface with clean paper or plastic sheet.

For painting

Brushes. A selection of good quality soft brushes size 0–6 are needed; also a small or medium-size stencil brush.

A palette. A plate or saucer can be used for mixing colours.

A sponge or piece of polyurethane foam. This is useful either for stippling or for applying larger areas of paint.

An iron. Most fabric paints need the application of heat in order to fix the colour permanently. Either a dry or a steam iron can be used.

A steamer. For specialist silk paints, this is necessary for fixing the colour. A home-made one can be constructed using a large saucepan or preserving pan with a lid **(78a)**.

For spraying

Various types of equipment can be used for spraying, their effectiveness generally depending on the price. However, for initial experiments it is not necessary to purchase an expensive air-brush and compressor.

A spray-gun. There is a wide range from which to choose, but a reasonably priced model to which you can attach a liquid air aerosol container works extremely well.

A mouth spray diffuser. This is a cheap and easy gadget which produces a less fine spray than a spray-gun.

A household or garden spray. These are good for spraying large areas.

A toothbrush and a knife. These can be used for more random spattering.

For stencils

A scalpel knife and a steel straight

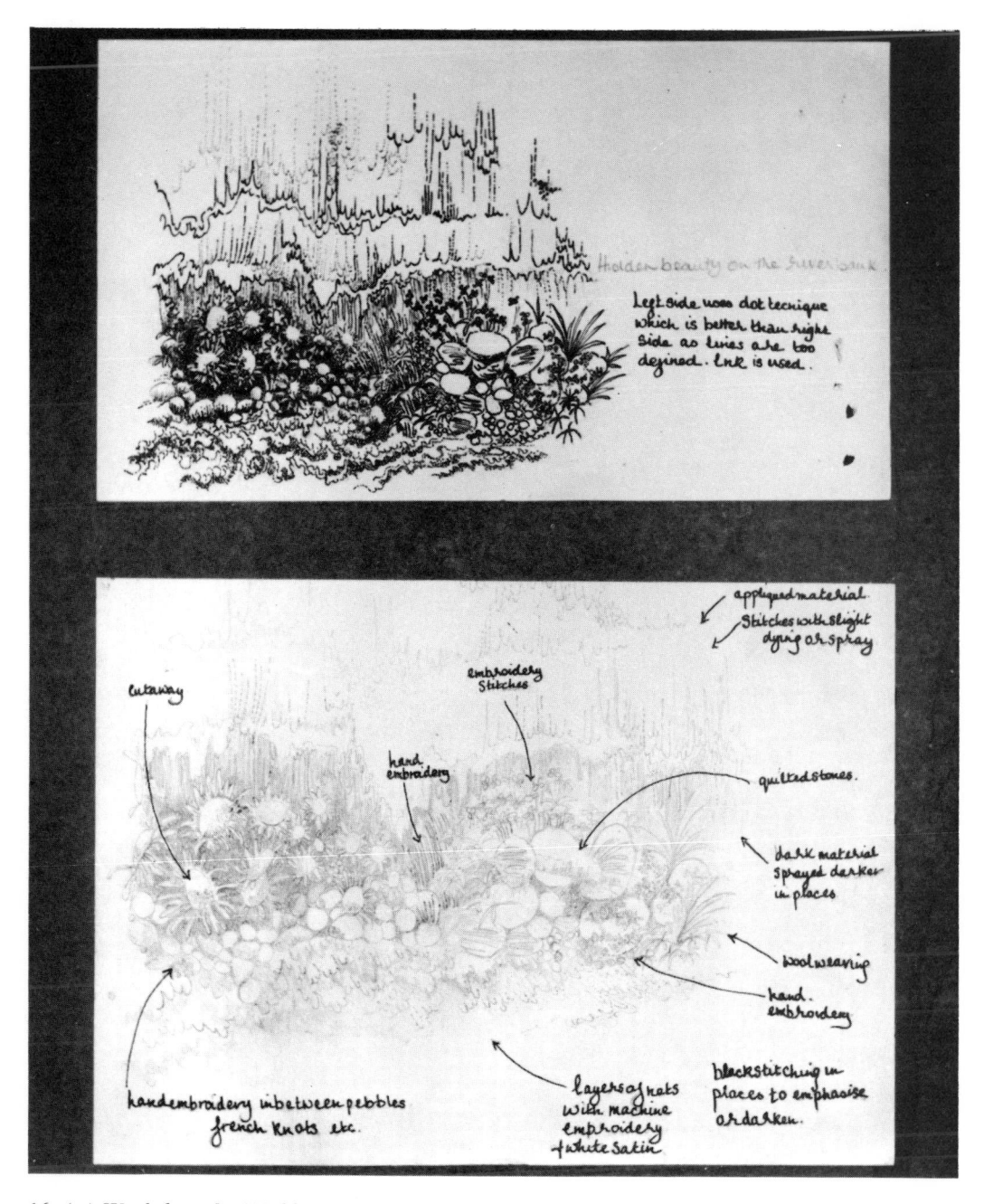

66 *(a) Worksheet for 'Hidden Beauty on the River Bank' by Julia Beevers*

(b) 'Hidden Beauty on the River Bank' by Julia Beevers: part of a very lushly embroidered panel incorporating a variety of techniques – spraying, machine and hand stitchery, appliqué and padding

82

edge. These are required for precise and accurate cutting of stencils.

Masking materials. Stencils can be cut from card, thick paper, stencil paper, acetate and self-adhesive protective film. Masking tape and newspaper are also useful.

Fabrics

Almost any type of cloth, natural or synthetic, can be painted, depending on the product used. For painting, smooth fabrics are best – avoid fuzzy or ridged material for the first experiments. Satin, though slippery, takes the colour well if painted with care. For spraying, very interesting effects can result on all types of fabric, both rough and smooth. New fabrics should be washed and ironed, before applying the paint, particularly if the article is to be worn or washed after use. If it is purely decorative, such as a hanging or picture, this may not be necessary. Silk and wool can also be painted with specialist dyes.

Paints

There are a number of fabric paints on the market, all of which give satisfactory results. They are very easy to use and generally can be

67 *(a) Worksheet for 'Seagulls' by Catherine O'Brien, using paper collage and spraying through a template*

made fast to washing and light by pressing with a hot iron. On garments or household articles of fine fabric, they are best used for small-scale painted designs, rather than for very large areas of colour – the paint does not penetrate the cloth as dye would, but remains on the surface, which means that if used too thickly, the resultant texture is rather stiff.

Specialist paints for silk and wool are available in a wide range of colours which can also be mixed together. They come in liquid form and produce a translucent water-colour effect, which does not affect the flexibility of the fabric. They are useful for garments, such as blouses and scarves, rather than for wall decorations, as they should not be permanently subjected to strong daylight.

(b) 'Seagulls' by Catherine O'Brien, a close-up of a larger panel. Layers of appliqué fabric in the foreground are complemented by a sprayed area, spattered with a mouth spray diffuser. The birds in the sky were printed from a block made by sticking a cut-out card shape on a piece of wood

84

Transferring the design

One of the methods described on page 63 should be used.

Painting method

Some fabric paints come ready mixed in the jar, which should be shaken, or the contents stirred well before use. Others need to be

68 '*Plant Study*' *by Mairead O'Riordan: appliqué and cut-work panel in satin, net and silk. The satin of the cyclamen flowers is freely painted and some areas are padded*

mixed first with a binder or extender, supplied with the paint. They are nearly all water-based and can be diluted if absolutely necessary with a little water, but it is advisable to add only the

69 *One fern leaf was repeatedly painted with fabric paint and printed directly on to heavy cotton*

minimum of water. If the solution is made too thin, it will be liable to seep along the grain of the fabric or flood into other parts of the design.

Secure, if possible, the previously ironed fabric to the working surface with masking tape. If the article to be painted is a garment, such as a T-shirt, insert a piece of card or heavy cartridge paper inside to protect the back. Otherwise the paint may seep through.

If practicable, always test the consistency and colour of the paint on a similar piece of fabric. Colours can be intermixed and added on top of one another; the possibilities are endless.

Start painting at the edge of an area and gradually fill in the shape. Allow one colour to dry thoroughly before adding another along-side or on top, unless you wish the colours to blend into one another.

Besides using various widths of brush, paint can be applied with a sponge or small piece of polyurethane foam to give a mottled effect. Allow the paint to dry. If working on a garment, remove the inserted protective paper before it is totally dry, to prevent it sticking to the design. Then cover the painted area with a clean cotton cloth or sheet of paper. Set the iron to as high a temperature as is practical for the fabric being used, and iron for several minutes, moving the iron from side to side. The article can then be washed and ironed if desired.

Leaf and fern prints **(69)** are effective.

Apply fabric paint thinly and evenly to the surface of the leaf and press it carefully down on to the stretched fabric. Potato prints can also be made by cutting a potato in half or into an interesting shape, painting the flat surface and pressing it firmly down on to the fabric. Wash all brushes and equipment in water immediately after use.

Spraying methods

It is necessary to mask or shield the areas which are not to be sprayed. This can be done with card, cartridge paper, masking tape, newspaper or self-adhesive film. The chosen masking material has to be cut to shape and taped in place during the spraying process. If spraying through a stencil, remember to mask the surrounding areas beyond the extremities of this **(70)**.

The selected paint should first be diluted to a thin enough consistency to flow satisfactorily through the spraying equipment. In most cases the best results are with a solution the consistency of milk, but this does vary with the type of gadget used. It is essential that the water is added very gradually, stirring all the time to eliminate any lumps, which would either block the spray outlet or cause blobs on the actual work. Mix up enough colour to complete the job, especially if you are intermixing colours.

Mouth spray diffuser

Staple or drawing pin the fabric to a frame and place in a vertical position. Having mixed the paint to a milky consistency, place the mouth-piece of the diffuser in your mouth and the other end in the paint, with the top outlet facing the work. Hold it about 15–20 cm (6–8 in.) away from the work. Take a deep breath and blow steadily and hard **(71)**. This method only takes a little practice to perfect.

Household/garden spray

This type of trigger-action spray also works best if the work is framed and placed in a vertical position. It is most useful for spraying

70 *Mask the area beyond the perimeter of the stencil, particularly when spraying*

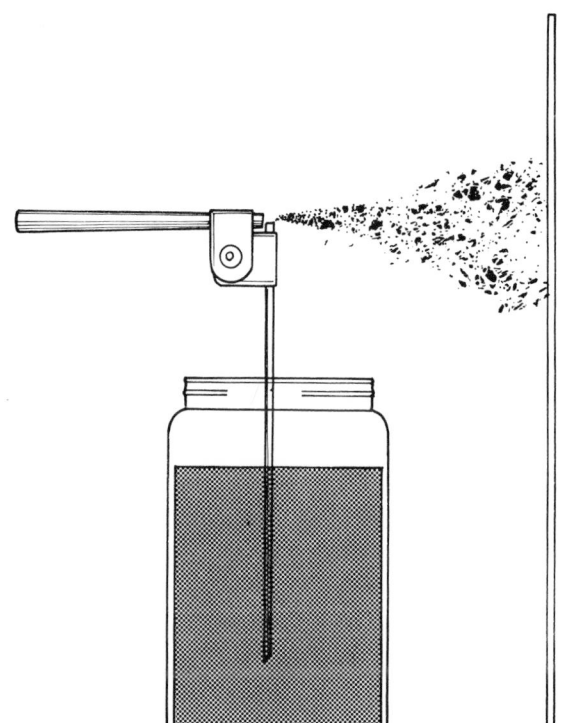

71 *Mouth spray diffuser – note that the work is placed in a vertical position*

72 *'Cluster of Plants' by Ann Cunnane. The outer areas of this appliqué and cutwork panel have been sprayed using a mouth spray diffuser. Layers of taffeta, furnishing fabrics, satin and net are machine embroidered*

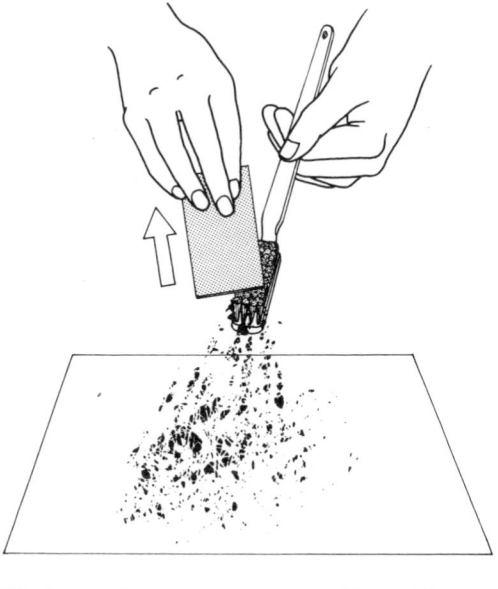

74 *Stencils must have each element of the design separated from its neighbour. The stencil brush has short stiff bristles which will help to force the paint between the fibres of the fabric*

73 *Spattering paint, using an old toothbrush and a piece of card*

large areas, as it is necessary to mix up at least 3 cm (1 in.) of liquid to cover the bottom of the container.

Toothbrush spattering

For this method the work can be in either a vertical or horizontal position, pinned to a frame or secured to the working surface with tape. Dip the toothbrush in the fabric paint – this does not usually need to be thinned. Holding the head of the brush away from you, take a piece of stiff card or a knife blade and draw it towards you over the bristles (73). With a little practice the paint can be accurately directed and will give the correct amount of coverage.

Spray-gun or air-brush

Most spray-guns and air-brushes work well if the work is placed in a horizontal position, so it can be taped to the working surface. The equipment should be attached either to a compressor for air, or to an aerosol contain-

ing air-brush propellant. Depending on the sophistication of the type of air-brush being used, various adjustments can be made to regulate the flow of paint. Mask all parts of the design that you do not wish to be sprayed, plus the surrounding areas (70). Hold the spray-gun 15–20 cm (6–8 in.) away from the surface and, using short strokes, move it constantly and at a steady rate, parallel to the surface. Do not spray too heavily. It is better to apply a light coat, then let it dry and respray.

Painting and spraying through a stencil

Stencilled designs have a quality of their own owing to the fact that each individual element is cut out and therefore separate from its neighbour. When the stencil is placed on the fabric and paint applied through the cut-out spaces, a fragmented stylized design will result (74).

Stencils of different types and designs, such as flowers, letters and geometric forms can be bought ready cut. However, these may not necessarily be suitable, either in size or pattern. Original stencils can be cut from card, mounting board, waxed stencil paper and

90

clear acetate. The design is drawn on to the selected masking material and each shape is cut out with a scalpel knife. It may be necessary to adjust the design to make sure that every element is separated from the next.

An alternative, which works extremely well on fabric, is self-adhesive film. This, which is the type sold for covering books etc., adheres to the fabric and so gives sharp and distinct outlines to the stencilled design. It is most

75 *A large red floor cushion by Elspeth Kemp which uses two hand-cut stencils. The design was inspired by a visit to Turkey where tulip shapes play a large part in traditional embroidery. The black fabric-painted shapes are further enhanced with machine-stitched lines of black tape*

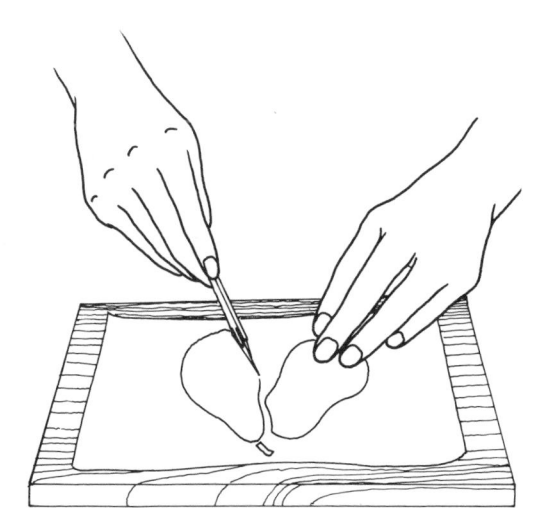

76 *Use a scalpel knife and cutting board for cutting out the stencil shapes*

satisfactory when used for small-scale work. The design must be drawn in reverse on the backing paper. The areas through which the paint is to be stencilled are then cut out with a scalpel knife. Use a cutting board or sheet of hardboard kept specifically for this purpose **(76)**. Peel off the protective backing paper and press the stencil down firmly on to the fabric which has been secured to the working surface. Make sure all the cut edges are securely adhered. For painting, use a stencil brush with your chosen fabric paint. Do not water this down unless absolutely necessary. Paint in the shapes with one or a variety of different colours, stabbing the brush down and forcing the paint between the fibres. Alternatively, use the stencil brush to produce a stippled or mottled effect. In this case, use the paint sparingly and hold the brush vertically, tapping it down gently through the holes in the stencil. Allow the paint to dry for a few minutes before peeling off the film. Wipe the stencil clean.

This and other types of stencil lend themselves readily to being used for repeat designs, as only one motif need be cut and the stencil can be positioned again for repainting. The transparency of the film allows you to be able

to register it correctly for subsequent use. These stencils can be used several times before the adhesive loses its effectiveness.

Paint can also be sprayed satisfactorily using self-adhesive film. Do not overspray or there will be a build-up of paint on the stencil which may drip on to the work as it is peeled off.

Silk paints

These paints are watery in consistency, giving a transparent colour. The liquid spreads by capillary migration along the fibres of the fabric. To enclose areas of colour, gutta resist (see below) is used to outline the shapes and this prevents the paint infiltrating other parts of the design.

Method

To transfer the design to the fabric, secure the drawing to the working surface, with the silk taped firmly on top, and trace through using a dotted pencil line. Then stretch the fabric, keeping the grain straight, either in a circular embroidery frame or on a rectangular wooden frame, using drawing pins to hold it fast.

If applying a background colour, this is best done with a large brush or sponge, working rapidly as the dye dries very quickly. For an even result use a wet sponge dipped in the dye and apply swiftly to previously dampened silk. Several colours can be merged to create water-colour style backgrounds, very suitable for further embellishment with embroidery.

For designs which call for specific areas to be painted in different colours, it is necessary

77 *A Mexican carving was the starting point for this stencil cut by the author from self-adhesive film and applied to the end of a scarf. The red and black painted design on grey woollen fabric is further embellished with needleweaving and hemstitching in red, black and white with matching fringe*

92

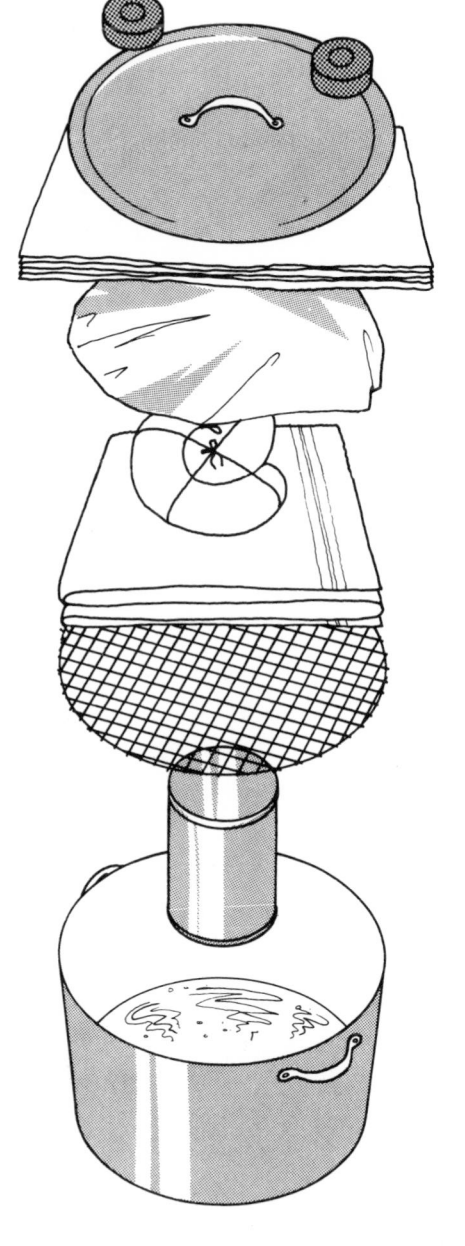

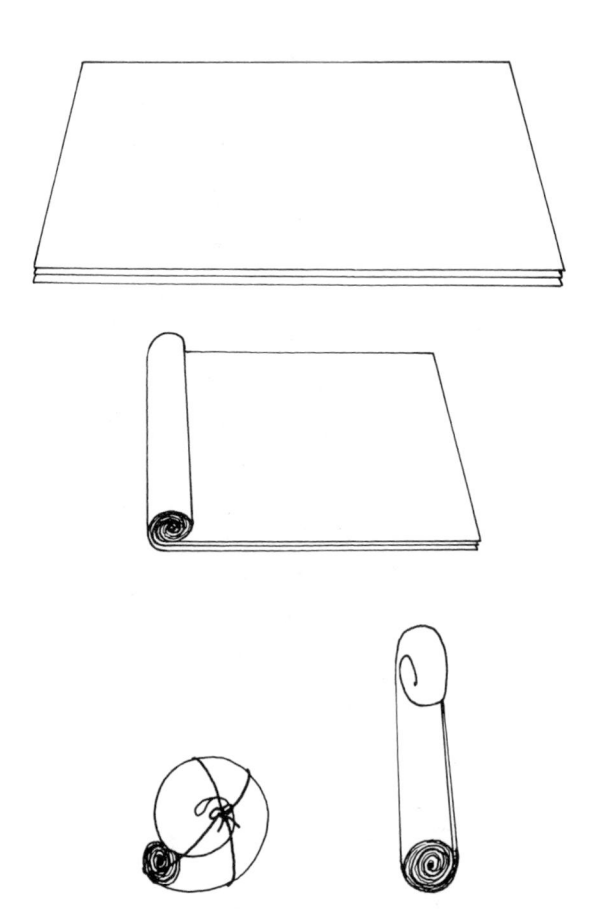

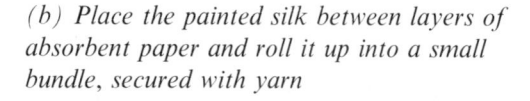

(b) Place the painted silk between layers of absorbent paper and roll it up into a small bundle, secured with yarn

to use gutta resist to enclose these shapes in order to prevent the paint flowing from one area to another. Gutta resist is available in clear, black, silver and gold and is a rubbery substance, best applied with a pipette – a small bottle with a tiny nozzle through which the gutta flows. It remains on the fabric giving a clear, black, gold or silver line. As with wax resist, it is imperative that the gutta penetrates through to the back of the fabric and so this method must totally enclose each shape. For heavy silks, dilute the gutta with a special dilutant. Allow the gutta to dry for about ten minutes and then use a small water-colour

78 Fixing silk dyes: (a) Construct a steamer using, from the bottom, a preserving pan, tin can, wire-rack, towel, painted silk rolled as in figure 78(b), tin foil, sheets of newspaper, lid and weights

94

brush to apply the paint within the enclosed areas. Each colour should be dry before continuing with the next. An unusual shimmering effect can be obtained if a small amount of salt is sprinkled on the wet surface and removed when completely dry.

With these silk paints, fixing is achieved by steaming. Although steamers can be purchased, a home-made one can be set up in the following way **(78a)**. Use a large saucepan or preserving pan with a lid, and pour in 5 cm (2 in.) of water and vinegar solution (three parts water to one part white vinegar). Construct a stand with a metal cylinder, such as a tin can with both ends removed, with a wire rack on top holding an old towel folded to absorb moisture. It is important that the painted silk does not come into contact with any drops of water, so it is placed between two sheets of absorbent paper (kitchen paper towel) and rolled into a bundle, small enough to fit on to the stand without touching the side of the steamer **(78b)**. Cover the bundle with a piece of tin foil, put several sheets of newspaper across the top of the steamer and replace the lid. Some heavy weights placed on the lid will help to hold it firmly in place and to build up steam pressure. Simmer gently for 45 minutes; then remove the silk and rinse in cool water. Iron dry with a cool iron.

Transfer paints and crayons

Transfer paints and crayons are useful for trying out ideas before committing the design to fabric. The design is painted or drawn on to paper and then ironed off on to fabric. Only synthetic fibres are suitable, and a number of colour experiments need to be made to ensure that the correct colour is transferred. It is a good idea to make a chart of the available colours before beginning a design, as the shades painted on the paper differ from those which result when transferred.

Fabrics

The transfer paints at present on the market have been developed primarily for use on synthetic fibres of the polyester/polyamide range (see Appendices I and II, pages 126, 127). However, some will work on linen, silk and cotton, and mixtures of natural and synthetic, but only with reduced shades. With man-made fibres, such as viscose rayon and acetate, the heat needed to transfer the paints is very high and care should be taken not to scorch or melt the fabric. If you are not sure of the fibre content of the fabric, tests should be made.

Method

Paint or crayon the design on to paper. A smooth non-absorbent paper is best for paints, a slightly rough cartridge for crayons. It is important to note that designs will be reversed when transferred to the fabric. Letters of the alphabet and numbers must of course be first drawn in reverse on to the paper **(80)**. If a slight error is made, or if there are smudges of paint or flecks of wax crayon around the design, these can easily be covered with masking tape. If the design is a motif, it can be cut out and pasted on to another piece of paper. Transfer paints should be allowed to dry for about 15 minutes; crayons can be used immediately. Cover the ironing table with several layers of newspaper and a final sheet of clean, white paper, and set the iron to the correct temperature for the fabric being used. Iron the fabric and carefully position the design face down on top. Over this, lay another sheet of clean white paper which is larger than the design. This will protect the iron, and also prevent the transfer slipping while it is being ironed. The length of time needed for ironing depends on the type of fabric, the heat of the iron and the depth of colour required. It is therefore advisable to do some preliminary tests. Move the iron steadily and firmly over the design until the transfer paper becomes slightly scorched and the

79 'Elderberries': this transfer print by the author in brown, green and purple was applied to mauve polyester crêpe. The leaves and stalks are outlined in backstitch and padded from the back; tiny black and iridescent beads and cream star stitches complete the effect (Courtesy Mrs Diane Berger)

80 When transferring letters or numbers, they must be painted on the paper in reverse

image shows through. Check that the design has transferred sufficiently by carefully lifting a corner. If not, iron for a little longer or increase the heat. The transfer can sometimes be used again with reduced effect, or it can be repainted.

Drawing

Alternatives to fabric paints can be tried with different effects. Some are only suitable for decorative panels or pictures as their fastness to washing is not guaranteed. They can be used in exactly the same way as on paper, but the fabric must be taped firmly to the working surface.

Felt-tip pens

These give good effects in a wide range of colours, particularly for line drawing, but should be checked for colour fastness to light. Experiment for flooded colour, either on wet fabric or on dry which is subsequently brushed with water.

Permanent pens

These are available in a small range of colours and are good for fine lines on most fabrics. They do, however, bleed on some materials on application.

Ball-point paint tubes

Available in 36 colours, including gold and silver, these are very good for line drawing on any fabric, and are washable and dry-cleanable (81). They need a little practice to manipulate, as the tube has to be held vertically and drawn across the fabric.

Instant shoe colour

This can be used on leather or plastic and comes in a good range of colours. The gold and silver can be used to add highlights on pictures.

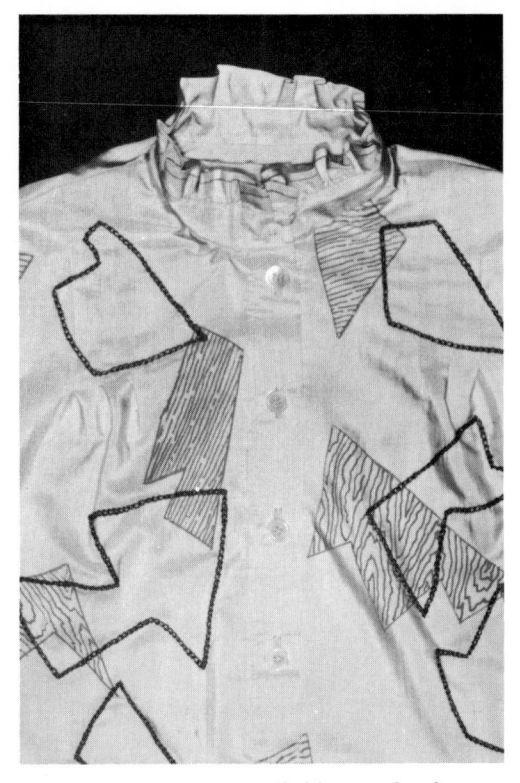

81 *Detail of a cream silk blouse; the design by Martin Brown is drawn with grey ball-point paint tubes. The chain stitch embroidery by the author re-iterates the drawn shapes*

Pastel dye sticks

Like wax crayon, these are rather difficult to apply evenly over large areas, but they give a soft pastel effect not otherwise obtainable (82). They are suitable for a range of fabrics, but for clear, bright colours choose a solid white or light-coloured background of natural fibres. For a permanent washable finish, cover the design with a sheet of clean paper and press with a hot iron. Rubbings can also be made – almost any hard textured surface which has a clear pattern in relief, such as carving, wooden fence, brickwork, embossed or engraved metal can be used. Work a small sample to start with, as large areas of fabric

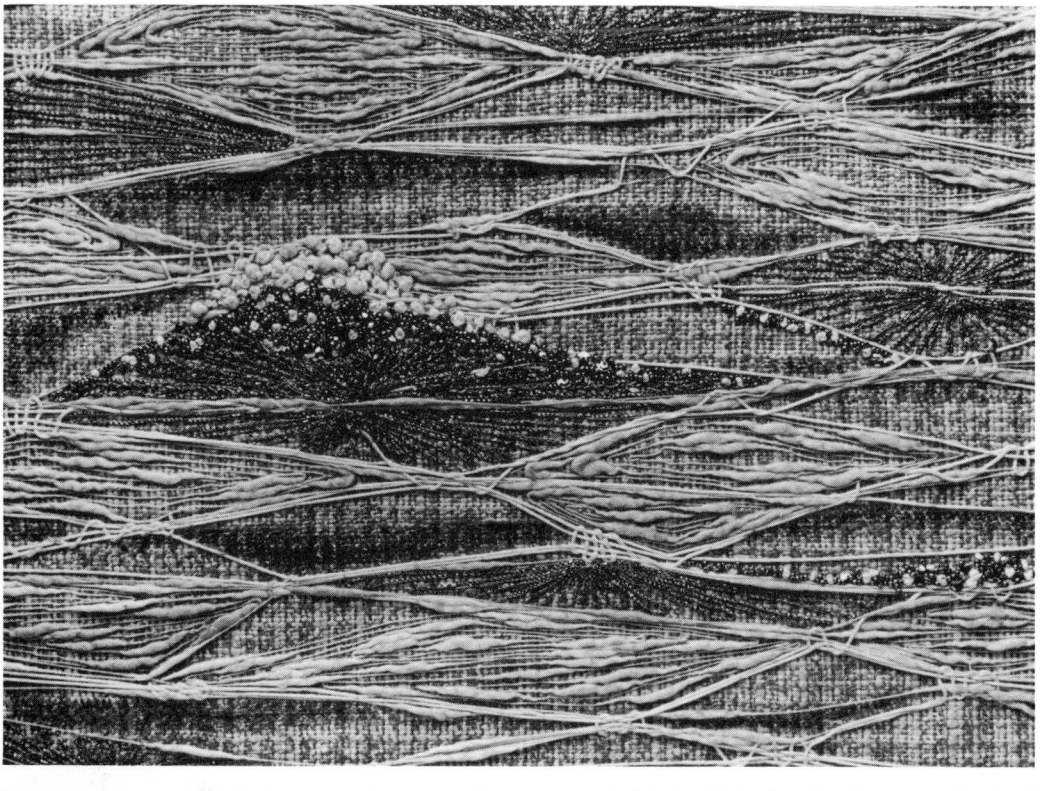

82 *Pastel dye sticks darken certain areas of the tweed background of this textured piece. The threads are mainly couched with loose needleweaving pulling the yarns apart to create irregular diamond shapes which are then ornamented with French knots and beads*

are difficult to hold firmly. Attach the fabric with masking tape to the surface to be rubbed. Using the pastel crayon on its side in order to cover a wide area, rub over the textured surface.

Experiments

Paints adding supplementary colour in embroidered pictures, garments and other articles can form either a major feature of the design or a subtle contribution to a background fabric. Painting is also a method of highlighting or outlining certain aspects of the work. Stencilled designs with their slightly fragmented quality give an individuality distinct from other types of painted decoration. This sort of motif would probably constitute the most prominent part of the ornamentation on a dress or household item. Some stencil designs have the same sort of application in terms of embroidery as those made with a tjap (see page 72) except of course that the batik design will be negative and the stencil method will have a positive result. As suggested with the tjap method, experiment with both repeat and border designs. Spraying also produces an effect which it is impossible to achieve in any other way. Because the paint has to be diluted, it is difficult to spray very dark colour. This, of course, can be turned to advantage, as the mistiness can be used to emulate shading in any number of ways **(83)**.

98

83 *Two similar samples showing spraying through and round a template, and through plastic mesh; the smaller design has been machine quilted*

By contrast, felt-tips, permanent pens and other drawing equipment can make a more definite mark by outlining a design in a different manner than can be done in stitchery.

Painting and spraying freehand or through a stencil

Decorative panels

Pictures for panels and wallhangings can be painted on fabric in the same way as any other picture, but it should be borne in mind that eventually embroidery will form part of the design. The considerations and their solutions are similar to those described for a batik picture (see page 79). The balance between paint and embroidery must be well proportioned, so that neither appears to overshadow the other and they combine harmoniously.

Attention to small detail in paint may not be necessary, as this can be achieved with the addition of texture or highlights in embroidery to specific areas. For landscapes, skies and other details only need be painted, and then the remainder worked in appliqué and stitches, somewhat emulating the eighteenth-century pictures of classical and pastoral scenes done in this way. Similarly, some areas of a canvaswork picture could be left unworked and the actual canvas painted (see colour plate 5).

99

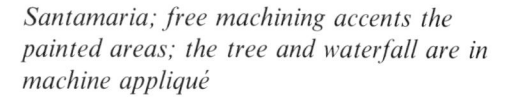

84 *Fabric paint and dye was applied to the previously dampened fabric to achieve the colour-washed effect of this panel by Pepa Santamaria; free machining accents the painted areas; the tree and waterfall are in machine appliqué*

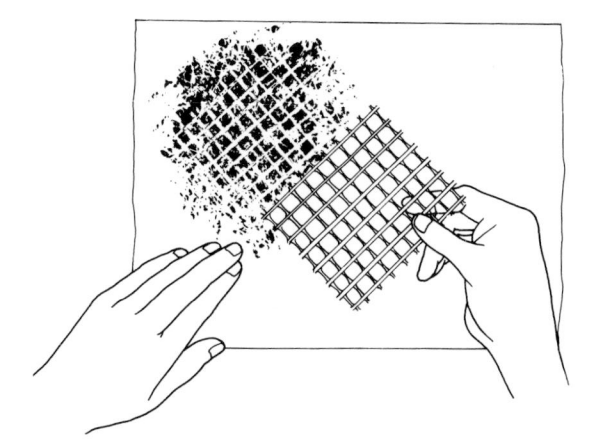

85 *Stippling through rug canvas for a trellis pattern*

86 *Rug canvas placed on the background before spraying gives a chequered design evoking a skyscraper skyline; this is then masked before re-spraying the sky. The foreground lace flowers are painted and outlined in cord*

Where a pastel background is needed, spraying is effective. Skies can be sprayed in a number of colours to depict all sorts of weather conditions from sunny to stormy. If spraying more than one colour, experiment initially by allowing the paint to dry between coats and then try spraying immediately while the first application is still wet. Shadows around embroidered motifs and reflections can either be spattered or sprayed.

Spraying or stippling through a variety of meshes **(85, 86)** provides another texture, a method which produces different sorts of negative images. Rug canvas as a mask gives a chequered pattern which can be used to represent buildings or brick walls, or placed diagonally it resembles trellis or lattice-work. The use of wire mesh of various sizes can depict pebbles, spots, paths etc. and gives a texture which can easily be included in an embroidered picture **(87)**. Felt-tip and permanent pens help to define a line or add shading. A simple line drawing could be enhanced with minimal stitchery, or a sketched landscape could create an idea for a contrasting panel combining drawing in the background, with heavily padded areas of interest in the foreground.

Garments

Painting or stencilling on dress can be outlined or accented in stitchery. For evening wear, painted velvet for a waistcoat would look superb with silk threads and beads. This could be combined with a handbag of similar fabric and embroidery. Chiffon, though not easy to handle, looks beautiful when sprayed, and silk can be used for a jacket with the painted design quilted. For day-time, exotic decoration is a less practical proposition, but blouses can be painted or have stencilled collars and cuffs, perhaps echoing a printed or woven pattern on a co-ordinating skirt. Leather and suede garments and accessories such as belts, buttons and handbags lend themselves to stencilled decoration, combined

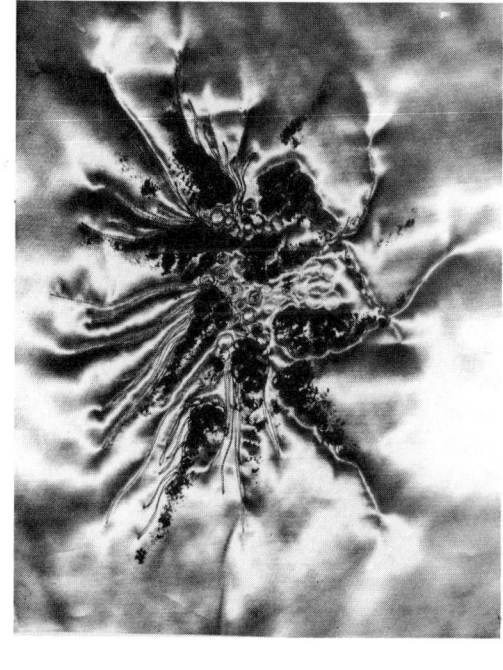

87 *'Brown Garden' by the author; a stencil brush with the minimum of paint was used to stipple the tree and vegetation; for the path, paint was stippled more heavily through a piece of wire mesh.* (Courtesy Mrs Iona Smith)

88 *A stippled design using fabric paint and stencil brush on shiny acetate material was quilted and machine stitched by Naomi Cohen-Ziv*

with appliqué or canvaswork. Sports clothes can have appropriate sporty motifs and beachwear any decoration from palm trees to sea-shells **(90)**.

Household items

For the home, cushions, tea-cosies, curtains and table linen can also be painted or sprayed. Spraying or stippling around objects **(91)** produces results similar to those obtained in

102

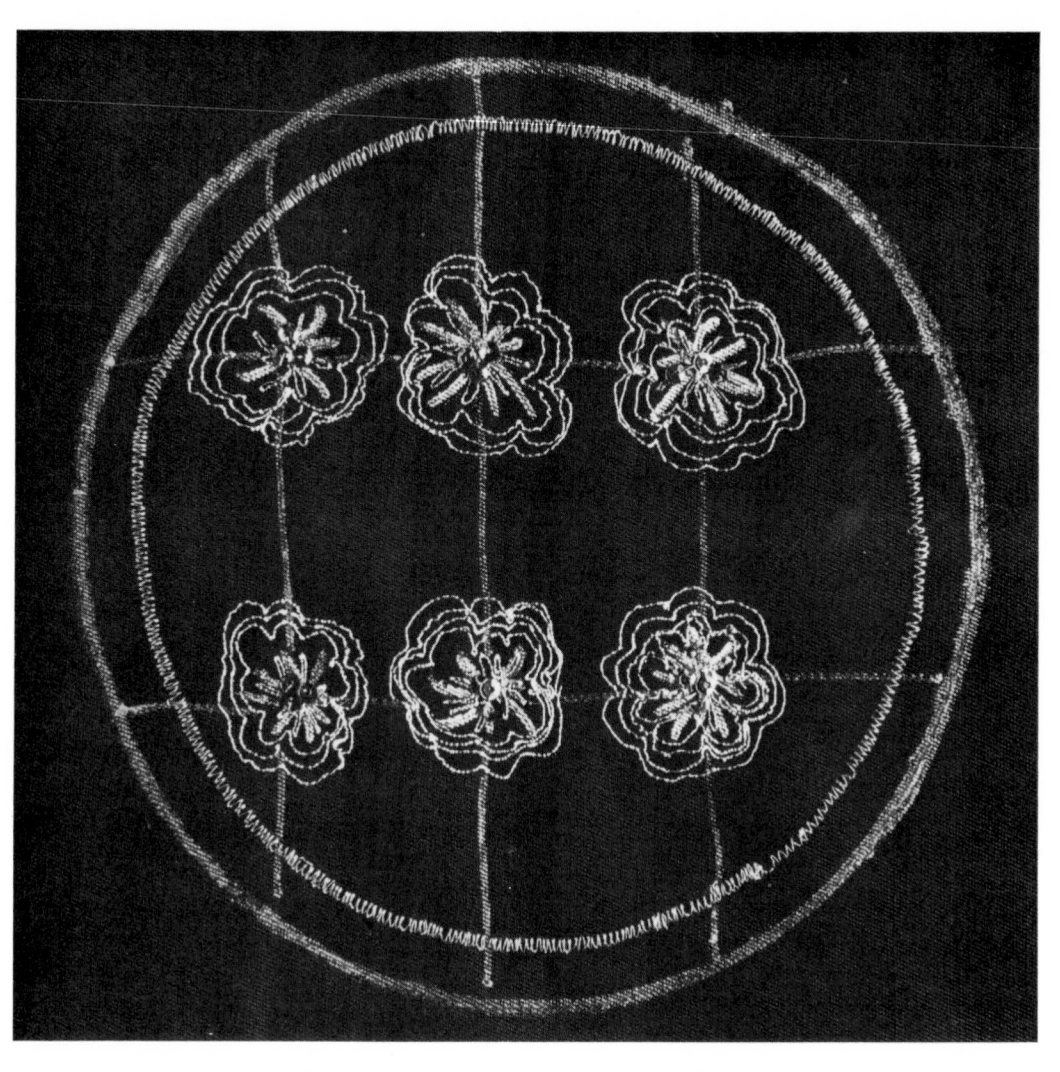

89 *A machine-embroidered motif in silver and black by Naomi Cohen-Ziv, suitable for a garment; the lines are drawn with ball-point paint tubes*

batik using the tjap method, that is a reverse image design. Formal or random patterns for interior design can be made by spraying round buttons, nuts and bolts, washers etc. Look for different-shaped items and try spraying them, or cut shapes in transparent film or in cartridge paper. Paper or card shapes can be attached to the fabric with double-sided adhesive tape. Masking tape also adheres well to fabric and is useful for geometric patterns, such as stripes, zig-zags or trellis patterns. Be careful also to mask all those surrounding areas which are not to be sprayed. Alternatively, ideas can often be taken from existing furnishings or objects in a room. Designs can be either realistic or stylized. If an individual motif is to be combined with embroidery, a simplified version will work successfully. For the kitchen, try painted or stencilled motifs of cups and saucers, fruit and vegetables, or a design adapted from that

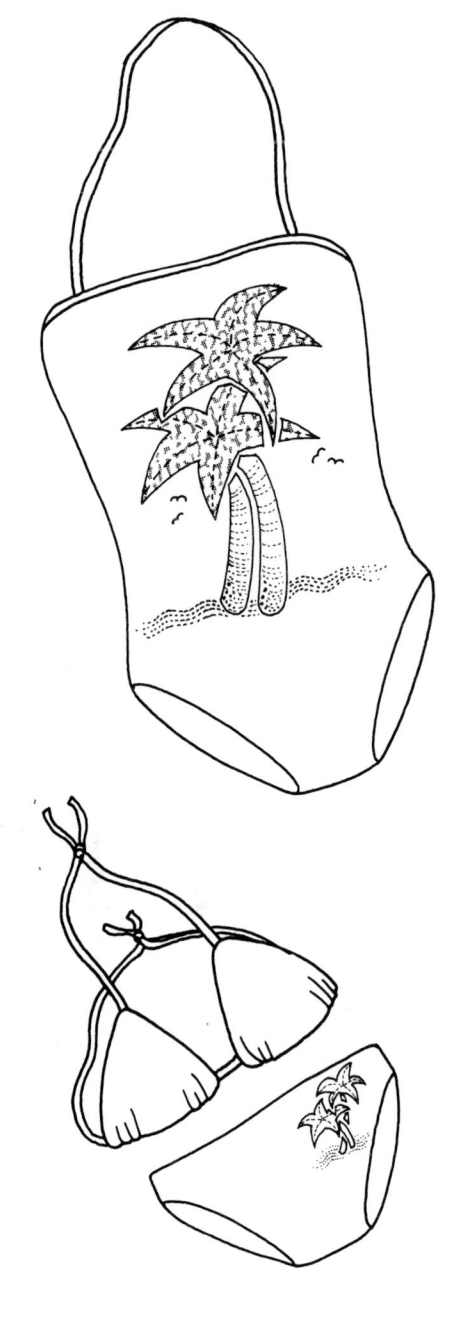

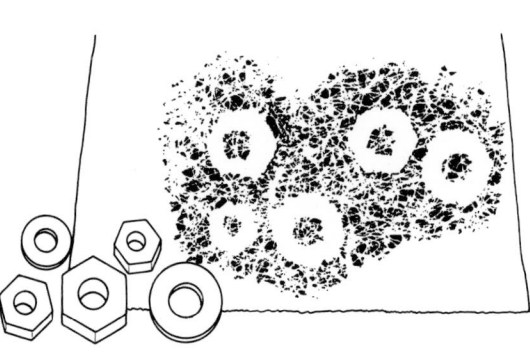

91 *Spraying round objects produces a negative image*

on the floor covering. Linen table mats with drawn thread hems could have mushroom or strawberry motifs painted along one side or in a corner. The same design could be used on a variety of quilted kitchen accessories such as oven-gloves or pot-holders, and covers for toaster, electric mixer etc.

For a living room, cushions could be derived from the carving on a piece of furniture or from an ornament. Certain aspects of existing textiles, carpet, curtains or wallpaper, should also be considered, either as a source of pattern or as a guide to your choice of colour. A co-ordinated scheme might consist of curtains painted in a large-scale design with some areas enhanced with machine embroidery, and matching cushions with a similar pattern on a smaller scale could be either hand-embroidered with a variety of textured threads or quilted. Bedroom furnishings can be either pretty or bold. Flowers can be painted or sprayed on quilts, and the bed-linen stencilled and embroidered with applied ribbons and dainty stitchery; or for a more striking effect the same items can have painted geometric shapes or stripes in bright colours decorated with machine embroidery.

Transfer printing

Transfer printing as a basis for further embroidery can be used in similar ways to those

90 *Painted shapes can be applied to beachwear either by hand or machine; or the design can be painted direct on to the garment and further decorated with stitchery*

92 *This simple flower design is a
combination of spraying and the use of ball-
point paint tubes; minimal stitchery fills in
spaces and co-ordinates the whole*

described for fabric painting. Its main limitation is that the fabric should be of synthetic fibres, though paler shades are possible on some others. This restriction may influence one's choice of usage. For example a satisfactory result would not be possible for a design for a child's calico dress which needed bright primary colours. The choice of fabric would

93 *A selection of potato prints on fabrics by Martin Brown; these can be quilted, used in patchwork or as a basis for hand or machine embroidery*

either have to be changed to something such as a polyester, in order to retain the colouring; or the same fabric could be used, but with a

106

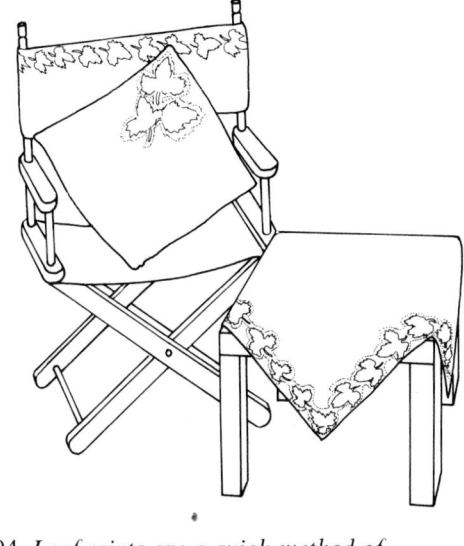

94 *Leaf prints are a quick method of applying decoration to household or garden furnishings*

pastel transfer-printed design.

Simple printing techniques, such as potato, leaf and grass prints are a quick and easy method of transfer printing, which require no actual drawing and give an extremely attractive result **(93, 94)**. Apply the transfer paint evenly to a piece of potato cut to an interesting shape, or a leaf, fern or grass. Press this firmly on to smooth paper and allow to dry, before ironing the print off on to the fabric.

Transfer crayons are especially good for rubbings. Experiment with anything that has a hard, slightly embossed surface in the same way as for pastel dye sticks (page 97). The paper rubbings can be cut out and reassembled, before transferring, to make unusual textured backgrounds suitable for decorating with embroidery.

6 EMBROIDERY TECHNIQUES

The most important consideration when combining extra colour in an embroidered work is the achievement of a well balanced design. The two techniques should integrate well, each playing its part to combine towards a successful composition.

The dyed or painted areas add colour, shape and line, the texture they produce being mainly in the form of pattern. The inherent textural quality of any form of embroidery added to a flat painted or dyed surface will give it another dimension. Simple stitches can reinforce lines, quilting will raise parts of the design, and beads will add highlights. Using hand-dyed fabrics for patchwork, appliqué or three-dimensional work will introduce a quality of pattern and colour unobtainable in commercially produced materials. The following embroidery methods will be familiar to most embroiderers and are those which will combine most readily with paints and dyes.

Stitches

For many people stitchery is synonymous with embroidery, and naturally plays a large part in enriching a work, by defining line and adding colour and texture. The combination of paint or dye with stitches is a very satisfactory one. Threads can be of any fibre: silk, wool, cotton, linen, metal or synthetic. Not only the specialist embroidery yarns are worth considering, but also knitting, crochet and weaving yarn, carpet thrums, string, jute, raffia, cords, ribbon, tape or strips of fabric. In fact, anything which can either be stitched or couched down. Threads all have different characteristics which may be rough or smooth, shiny or dull, hairy, soft or knobbly. Together they can be juxtaposed for contrasting texture or, used alone, they bring unity to a composition. They can be used singly or doubled, the ply can be separated in some yarns, or different types can be combined and used as one. Of course, your choice of thread much depends both on the aesthetic aspect of the design and on the practical considerations with regard to its use.

Panels and wallhangings present few barriers in terms of either selection of thread or of

95 'The Fishmongers' by Julia Beevers: a detail of a panel which incorporates a number of techniques; the background is batik 'crackle' fabric whilst some parts of the applied shapes have been shaded with paint. Scrim, hessian, cotton, linen and net are machine appliquéd for a lively composition

the type of stitch. Garments and useful articles have to be assessed individually. Stitches with long loose threads would not be suitable for children's wear or table linen and some threads are not washable or would be too rough for comfort on a garment.

Hand stitches

Stitches can be meticulously worked in a traditional way, or adapted and modified to create new ideas, patterns and textures. When integrating stitches in a painted and dyed design, *stitches which produce lines*, either delicate or bold, are essential for outlining or emphasizing a shape **(96)**. The most useful of these are the following:

> back stitch
> chain stitch
> coral stitch
> couching
> double knot stitch
> Portuguese stem stitch
> running stitch
> stem stitch
> scroll stitch
> twisted chain stitch
> whipped chain stitch

Single unit stitches which give an overall pattern or texture can be superimposed on coloured or sprayed areas in either toning or contrasting thread. Those falling into this category are:

> detached chain
> detached wheatear
> ermine filling
> fly stitch
> seeding
> star filling
> tête-de-boeuf filling

These are sufficiently open and spaced out not to cover the coloured area. They can help to lighten a shape which may be too dark, or add strength to a weak area of tone.

Similarly, *open textured filling stitches* such as those used in needlemade lace, based on detached buttonhole stitch, can be sewn over a painted or dyed area without concealing its colour **(32)**; try also cloud filling, open wave and lattice stitches based on an open grid of crossing threads.

Alternatively, *solid areas of stitchery* in Bokhara or Roumanian couching, long and short stitch or satin stitch add variety of texture and tone to a painted fabric, contrasting sharply with the flat coloured surface.

Knotted stitches and those producing dots or circular motifs are very versatile and create a large number of effects. They include:

> buttonhole and woven wheels
> eyelets
> French, Chinese and bullion knots
> raised cup stitch
> rosette chain circles
> spider's webs

These can be closely stitched for a heavy knobbly texture or powdered lightly over a wide area.

Borders and band stitches combine well with dyed materials. Stripes of the following stitches all give interesting contrasting texture in dress and household articles, particularly those in more formal patterns:

> braid stitch
> chevron stitch
> herringbone stitch
> open Cretan stitch
> raised chain band
> rosette chain stitch

96 'Iris' waistcoat in pure wool crêpe painted *and made by the author. Self adhesive acetate film was used as a mask before painting the stencil. The design is quilted by couching with a double line of cotton perle*

110

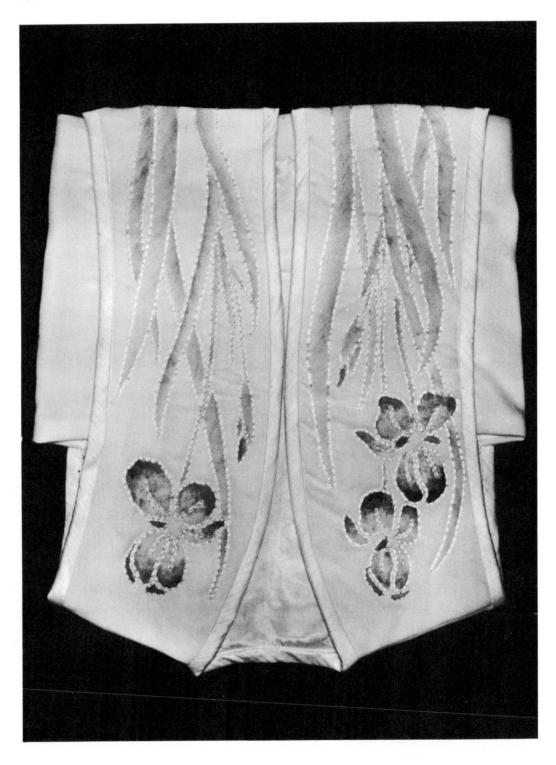

Machine stitching

The automatic sewing machine used for embroidery can add areas of pattern or alter a tone or shape in a similar way to hand stitchery, if the foot is removed and the fabric framed for free machining. Although free machine embroidery takes a certain amount of practice to perfect, whip stitch and free satin stitch give delicate effects which are easy to achieve. Cable stitch, which produces a thicker line, is best used on tie-dyed or batik pieces, as it has to be worked from the wrong side of the fabric with the heavier thread, such as cotton perle, wound on the spool. Satin stitch blobs and machine eyelets create areas of texture. In addition, interesting thick or knobbly wools can be couched down either by free machining or using the presser foot. The decorative embroidery stitches on many modern automatic sewing machines can be used in the same way as the hand-stitched border and band stitches described above (98).

97 'Seascape' by Sian Kibblewhite: a batik panel with the central area heavily machine embroidered and some parts of the foreground accentuated with light machining

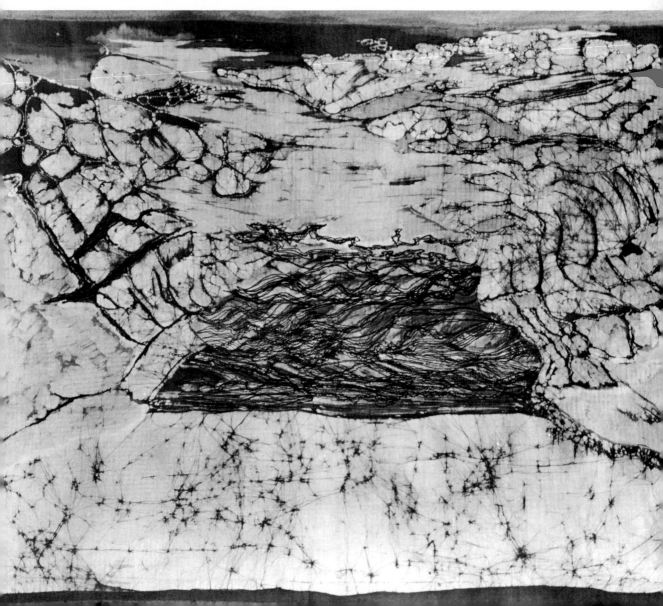

Quilting

Quilting can be very successfully combined with paints and dyes as it gives texture without additional colour. Smooth fabrics such as silk, satin, cotton or fine suede and leather all quilt well. The three main quilting techniques of English, Italian and trapunto can be used separately or together, and in conjunction with surface stitches or beads.

English (or wadded) quilting

This produces an overall padded effect made by sandwiching a layer of wadding between

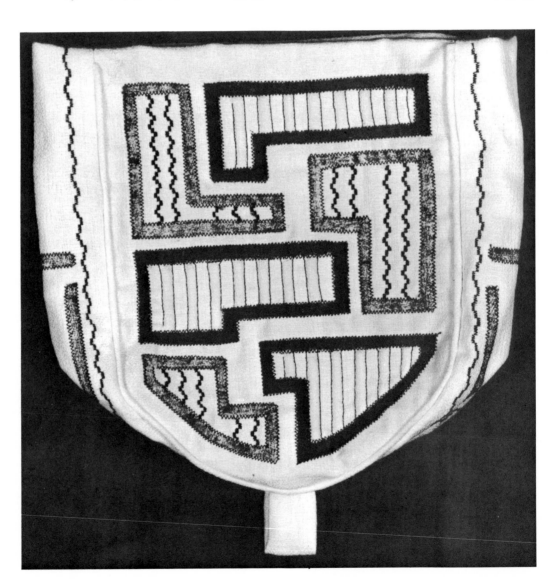

98 *The geometric stencil design on this teacosy has been painted solidly in some areas and stippled lightly in others for a variation in tone. Texture and pattern are added with Italian quilting and automatic machine embroidery stitches*

or appliqué could be surrounded with a padded frame.

A dyed or painted pattern will look best if quilted in a thread which matches the background fabric or picks out the colouring of the design. In this case the actual stitches, though they should be neatly and evenly executed, are unimportant to the look of the work, and serve merely to hold the layers together to create the decorative padded effect. Only the main outlines and maybe one or two other important lines need be worked, to separate the painted area from the background. Alternatively, the whole of the plain area could be flattened by covering with geometric or random wavy lines of stitching. This will lift the painted image into relief. A pattern of seeding, little stab stitches dotted at different angles over the entire background surface, serves a similar purpose.

Use a cotton or silk thread, or buttonhole twist, and work with even stitches. Back stitch will define the outline crisply, stab stitch less so. A chain or other decorative stitch such as stem would impose itself more on the design, which might detract from the painted or dyed motif, particularly if it is small in scale. However, in cases where a bold outline is needed, or a weakness in the painted design needs to be disguised, a heavy stitch will be best.

Italian (or corded) quilting

This method is particularly good for outlining or accentuating certain linear aspects of a design. On a double layer of fabric, two parallel lines of back stitch are worked. A large-eyed tapestry needle containing quilting wool or thick knitting wool is then inserted into the backing fabric and threaded between the lines of stitching, making sure that the needle does not pierce the top fabric. Tjanting lines in a batik picture or outlines in tritik can both be raised in this way. Celtic and interlaced designs, and those with flowing lines, for instance in Art Nouveau or classical style,

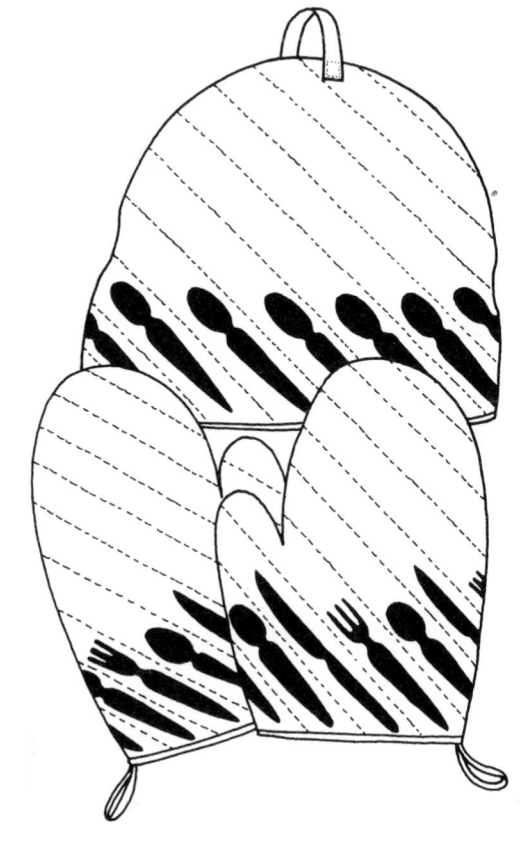

99 *Small kitchen accessories can have simple motifs painted and quilted*

the top fabric and the backing, and then stitching a design through all three layers. It is widely used for cushions, quilts and even bedheads; also small kitchen accessories such as tea and coffee cosies and oven-gloves **(99)**. All over repeat patterns made with a tjap or stencil are suitable. Garments such as jackets and waistcoats can be entirely quilted or have details on pockets and cuffs painted and padded. This method can also be introduced in wallhangings to raise some part of the design. In a painted landscape, the foreground could be quilted and the focal point of a motif or abstract design emphasized in a similar way. An embroidered picture in canvaswork

114

resemble the furrows of a ploughed field, or ripples on a stretch of water. Garments can be enhanced with several lines of raised texture stitched to add weight to cuffs or hems. Painted or transfer-printed satin cushions look very effective with some areas outlined with these raised channels, and geometric designs can be given an added texture of a formal ridged effect. It is usual to stitch with a

lend themselves to this method (101). Italian quilting would also form an area of embossed texture on an embroidered panel, which might

100 Hand-quilted silk cushion by Ann Holland; the design is sprayed through a template with French knots massed together emphasizing the central area and reflecting some shapes

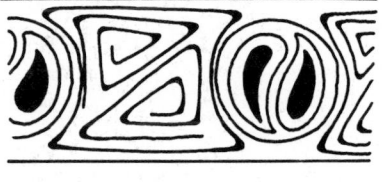

101 *Celtic and interlaced designs are suitable for Italian quilting*

matching or toning thread; for a clean, crisp line use a double row of back stitch or straight machine stitch. If using the sewing machine, a twin or double needle can also be used to make a narrow channel. Some sewing machines have a pin-tuck attachment which, with the double needle and a gimp underneath, produces an effect similar to Italian quilting.

Trapunto (or stuffed) quilting

For an area in a painted or dyed design which needs to be raised whilst the background remains flat, Trapunto quilting is the solution. This gives a similar effect to Italian quilting, but one is not restricted to padding only in lines – enclosed shapes of almost any design can be stuffed. Using a double layer of fabric, the shape to be padded is surrounded with a single row of back or machine-stitching. A small slit is then carefully made in the backing fabric and the shape gently stuffed with Terylene wadding. The gap is then sewn up and the padded area will stand out in relief. Motifs which have been painted or stencilled or those made with a tjap can all be padded successfully, or the focal point of a quilted picture or abstract design can be raised in high or low relief.

Appliqué

Applying fabrics to a background has many practical as well as decorative uses, adding shape, pattern, colour and texture to a design. It can enhance both children's and adults' clothes and adds individuality to interior design schemes. Hand-painted and dyed fabrics in particular give a new dimension to your work, either stitched on a plain background or vice versa. The choice of fabric, natural or synthetic, for an appliquéd article must be appropriate to its use. For dress and household items, the suitability of the fabric with regard to practical considerations and comfort is of foremost importance. Children's wear obviously needs to be hardwearing and washable, a glamorous evening gown with silk batik motifs need not. For decorative panels, the selection of fabrics largely depends on their visual aspect, and with the advent of iron-on and bonding interlinings, the necessity to apply fabrics only on the straight grain has largely been eliminated. This of course makes it very easy to use off-cuts of interestingly patterned dyed or painted materials. Fabrics which do not fray are very often chosen for appliqué, as there is no need to turn under a hem. Felt does not dye satisfactorily,

116

but can be painted; washable gloving and shirting in suede or leather can be tie-dyed very effectively and could decorate a picture, garments or accessories, such as handbags or belts. Interlinings like Vilene dye and accept paint well and can also be used for appliqué (see front cover). They are available in a variety of thicknesses and qualities.

102 'Coronation Street' by Pepa Santamaria. The lower roof tiles are trapunto-quilted hand-dyed cotton; other fabrics include scrim, wool and curtain lining, all machine embroidered

Shapes for appliqué should be fairly bold in concept – narrow or complicated areas, particularly those with sharp corners, are difficult to apply and are best avoided, unless a non-fraying fabric is being used. As you can colour the fabric exactly as you wish, it is easy to

103 The sprayed background for this appliqué panel by Pepa Santamaria is a delicate foil for the bold print of the curtains: details are added with hand and machine stitches

obtain harmonizing tones simply by dyeing a selection of different materials, without even using any of the resist processes. A panel with a painted, tie-dyed or batik background can have plain-dyed toning or contrasting fabrics added. You can exploit the tie-dye pattern made, for example, by tying up buttons and stones, for a large area of applied background, or the fabric can be cut up and each motif used individually. Striped ikat designs create linear pattern for appliqué landscapes or abstract designs. Fragments of otherwise un-

104 *Appliqué is a very suitable medium for creating simple, bold effects in playroom or nursery*

and if machined is quick to do and hard-wearing. This makes it particularly suitable for children's wear. Even simple items such as T-shirts can have dyed appliqué motifs added – a tiger in tie-dyed or tritik stripes or a batik motif based on natural forms. Use similar ideas to exploit the inherent boldness of appliqué with pictorial designs for furnishings in playroom or garden **(104)**. Dyed ribbons, tapes and cords can be used for trimming.

Beads

Beads can add highlights or texture to a dyed or painted picture and to garments. They come in every colour, shape and size imaginable from tiny seed pearls to large wooden or china lozenges. Some are faceted and round, others smooth and long. Baubles and other jewels are also available. These, in particular, give a theatrical appearance to a work, but need to be used with sensitivity or the effect will be garish. Glass beads and sequins, traditionally used to add sparkle to evening wear, incorporate well with luxury fabrics such as chiffon, georgette, satin and velvet, all of which take paint and dye beautifully. They can look at their most exciting if massed together in groups, perhaps at the centre of a batik design **(105)**; or gradually diminishing in number from a cluster to a scattering over a sprayed area. They could well be used in a similar way to emphasize the focal point of an abstract tie-dyed panel, or a batik picture in which the beads could reinforce the design made with tjanting dots. For a more rugged effect, wooden beads, round, oval or square, integrate well with wool, tweed, linen or hessian, which can be sprayed or painted. They can also be used effectively with painted and dyed leather or suede for a rough, shaggy wallhanging.

A beading needle and waxed thread will be needed for tiny glass beads; others can be attached using any needle which will go

interesting dyed fabric can often be used for small areas of appliqué which might require a different pattern or texture. Parts of an appliqué picture can be painted or transfer printed, either before or after the fabric is attached. Use organza, net or chiffon to soften a too harshly toned background or to create a misty effect. An unattractively dyed sample can be altered with the addition of transparent fabrics. They can be sprayed, painted or dyed to give a wealth of new ideas.

Padded appliqué in an appropriately dyed colour or pattern can elevate the focal point of a design or the foreground of a picture. Three-dimensional shapes can be added – try leaves in painted or tie-dyed leather and suede attached to a tree design; geometric stencil or tjap designs cut out and glued or laced over a card template could make a striking panel in high or low relief. Appliqué on dress is a very attractive decoration. It transforms a plain garment into something special and unusual,

120

106 *Two ways of applying beads: on the left a number of beads threaded to make a loop; on the right, beads stitched in stalk formation*

105 Opposite *A silk batik sample showing a two-colour brush and tjanting design with one end emphasized with china beads and textured threads*

through the hole. They can be sewn on singly, or threaded in rows and couched down. An alternative is to use a tambour hook to attach long rows of beads and sequins. A way of achieving greater texture is to thread several beads and re-insert the needle back into almost the same spot on the fabric **(106)**. The result will be a loop of beads which will stand up. If this process is repeated many times in a closely massed group, a thickly encrusted texture will evolve. To make a little raised stalk or stamen, two or three beads are threaded and the needle taken back into the same hole, passing again through all except the top bead **(106)**.

Patchwork

The art of patchwork depends very much for its effect on the selection of fabric. The interplay of light and shade, pattern and colour needs careful consideration. So often one sees a patchwork item neatly made but with an ill-considered choice of materials. Dyeing your own fabric can offer a way of ensuring an overall effect of toning colours. A range of different printed off-cuts put in a dye-

bath will result in a collection of blending fabrics.

Home-dyed materials have an entirely different quality from those commercially produced – they have a certain softness and luminosity unlike shop-bought fabrics which have a clearer, crisper hue. Using your own dyed fabrics with these needs some thought to ensure that they harmonize properly. However, some, including calico, combine well.

Fibres can be of any sort which will paint or dye successfully. Different types can be used together provided that they are of similar weight. Indeed, the contrast between dull and shiny surfaces, or those of different texture, is an added attraction. Fabrics for patchwork can be specially tie-dyed, batiked or painted, and off-cuts from appliqué or discarded ex-

107 *A painted and quilted butterfly forms the central square of a log-cabin patchwork cushion*

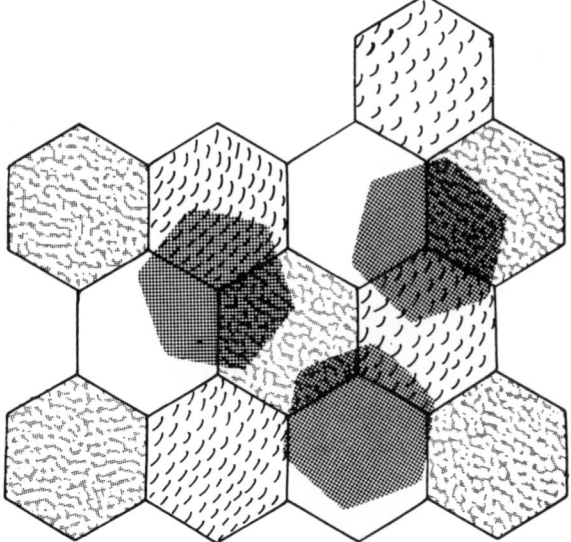

108 *Patchwork can incorporate paints and dyes; hexagons with painted flower motif, tjanting or tritik dots or sprayed perimeters to the patches. The second example shows how areas can be sprayed or painted through a template to reflect or alter the shapes. A log cabin design can have an appliqué shape of painted or dyed fabric for the central square*

periments are also useful. If including batik or painted motifs in a work, a successful balance will be achieved by including a larger proportion of plain-coloured fabrics as opposed to printed. A template design of plain hexagons or squares could have some patches decorated with a painted or batik motif such as a flower or leaf. A child's patchwork quilt might have trains, cars or animals painted round the border, or tie-dye forming a pattern in the centre. The central square or rectangle

of log-cabin can contain painted decoration (**107**) as can the inserted pieces in the cathedral window method. The seams of a patchwork article can be emphasized or reflected by outlining either by painting or drawing; tritik lines can follow those of a patched design made in Suffolk puffs, clamshell or template method. Seminole patchwork can incorporate striped brushed batik or stencilled fabric.

Manipulating fabrics

Altering the existing textural quality of a fabric presents exciting new opportunities for creative work. With the addition of painting and dyeing, the possibilities are endless. Ex-

124

periment with any method which changes the flat quality of a fabric, either by pulling, folding, gathering, pleating, smocking, tucking or ruching. All types of fabric can be manipulated in some manner, and the inherent quality of the fibres should be exploited. Soft materials, such as georgette and crêpe, ruche beautifully, as does chiffon velvet and soft gloving leather. These, however, would be difficult to pleat or tuck, except in unpressed folds. In contrast, crisp fabrics like poplin, silk, linen and silk organza can be pleated and tucked very precisely.

The manipulated fabric can be included in some decorative way on a garment or other article, or applied to an embroidered panel, to create interesting texture. Smocking has been traditionally used on costume, and specially dyed or painted fabric incorporates effectively in a design. A smocked garment looks beautiful if sprayed or ombré dyed – a gathered tritik pattern would translate easily into a smocked yoke. It is possible also to amalgamate this method in an unusual textured area for a wallhanging or picture.

Tucks and pleats can be used on painted, stencilled or tjap designs for household or decorative use. They can be precisely stitched for a formal geometric effect or made unevenly in different widths for a more random area of relief. Dyed chiffon or organza ruched or gathered haphazardly is easy to manipulate and can be attached within a space with small invisible stitching, keeping the turning in place and controlling the ruching. Tights dipped in dilute bleach and then redyed can also be cut up and ruched, gathered or draped for an unusual texture.

109 *This unusual waistcoat by Linda Brassington exploits the contrast between dyed and undyed fabrics; the bodice combines dyed calico pieced with unbleached calico; the pleated collar has a wax resist design made with a tjap of strip aluminium mounted on wood* (Photo: Simon Sleigh)

APPENDIX I

Fabric categories

Natural fibres

Vegetable – *Cotton, linen*
Animal – *Wool, silk*

Manmade fibres (from natural sources)

Cellulose – *Viscose Rayon: Evlan, Raycelon, Sarille, Vincel*

Cellulose Ester – *Acetate: Dicel, Lansil, Tricelon, Tricel*

Synthetic fibres (from chemical sources)

Polyamides – *Banlon, Bri-nylon, Celon, Enkalon, Enkasheer, Nylon, Nyltest, Perlon, Tendrelle*

Polyesters – *Crimplene, Dacron, Diolen, Tergal, Terlenka, Terylene, Trevira*

Acrylics – *Acrilan, Cashmilon, Courtelle, Dralon, Leacril, Neospun, Orlon*

Glass fibre

APPENDIX II

Suitability of fabrics for painting and dyeing

Fabric	Hot-water dye	Cold-water dye	Fabric paint	Transfer paint
Acetate	√	×	√	×
Acrilan	×	×	√	×
Banlon	√	×	√	√
Bri-nylon	√	×	√	√
Canvas	√	√	√	√ (R)
Cashmere	×	×	√	√ (R)
Cashmilon	×	×	√	×
Celon	√	×	√	√
Cotton	√	√	√	√ (R)
Courtelle	×	×	√	×
Crimplene	√ (R)	×	√	√
Dacron	√ (R)	×	√	√
Dicel	√	×	√	×
Diolen	√ (R)	×	√	√
Dralon	×	×	√	×
Enkalon	√	×	√	√
Enkasheer	√	×	√	√
Evlan	√	√	√	×
Fibreglass		×	√	×
Helanca	√	×	√	√
Lansil	√	×	√	×
Leacril	×	×	√	×
Linen	√	√	√	√ (R)
Neospun	×	×	√	×
Nylon	√	×	√	√

Fabric	Hot-water dye	Cold-water dye	Fabric paint	Transfer paint
Nyltest	√	×	√	√
Orlon	×	×	√	×
Perlon	√	×	√	√
Polyester and mixtures	√ (R)	√ (R)	√	√
Raycelon	√	√	√	×
Sarille	√	√	√	×
Silk	√	√ (R)	√	×
Tendrelle	√	×	√	√
Tergal	√ (R)	×	√	√
Terlenka	√ (R)	×	√	√
Terylene	√ (R)	×	√	√
Trevira	√ (R)	×	√	√
Tricel	√ (R)	×	√	√
Tricelon	√	×	√	√
Vincel	√	√	√	×
Viscose Rayon	√	√	√	×
Washable leather	×	√	√	√
Wool	√	√	√	×

(R) = reduced shades only

SUPPLIERS

Great Britain

Equipment, dyes and paints

Berol Ltd
Oldmedow Road
King's Lynn
Norfolk PE30 4JR
Fabricol and Fabritint colours

Binney & Smith (Europe) Ltd
Ampthill Road
Bedford MK42 9RS
Fabricrayons

Candlemakers' Supplies
28 Blythe Road
London W14 OHA
Tie-dye and batik materials, Procion M dyes, Deka transfer paints and permanent fabric paints

Dryad
P.O. Box 38
Northgates
Leicester LE1 9BU
Tie-dye and batik materials, fabric paints

Dylon International Ltd
Lower Sydenham
London SE26 5HD
Dylon dyes, Colour-Fun Fabric paints, Dygon colour remover

London Textile Workshop
65 Rosebery Road
London N10
Russell Dye System for wool, chemical and natural dyes.

George Rowney & Co. Ltd
P.O. Box 10
Bracknell
Berkshire RG12 4ST
Rowney Screen and Fabric Printing colours

George Weil & Sons Ltd
63–65 Riding House Street
London W1P 7PP
Super Tinfix Silk paints, Procion M dyes, silk and cotton fabrics

Winsor & Newton
Whitefriars Avenue
Wealdstone
Harrow
Middlesex HA3 5RH
Printex Fabric Printing colour

Fabrics

John Lewis
Oxford Street
London W1
and branches
A large selection of dress and furnishing fabrics of all fabric categories

129

Whaleys (Bradford) Ltd
Harris Court
Great Horton
Bradford
West Yorkshire BD7 4EQ
A wide range of silks and cottons, many ready prepared for dyeing or painting

General embroidery supplies

The Camden Needlecraft Centre
High Street
Chipping Camden
Gloucestershire

de Denne Ltd
159–161 Kenton Road
Kenton
Harrow
Middlesex

John Lewis
Oxford Street
London W1
and branches

Mace & Nairn
89 Crane Street
Salisbury
Wiltshire

Royal School of Needlework
25 Princes Gate
London SW7

The Silver Thimble
33 Gay Street
Bath
Avon

USA

Equipment, dyes and paints

Aiko's Art Materials Import Inc.
714 N. Wabash Avenue
Chicago
Illinois 60611
Dyes and batik materials

Cerulean Blue Ltd
P.O. Box 21168
Seattle
WA 9811
All batik and dyeing materials and equipment

W. Cushing & Co.
North Street
Kennebunkport
Maine 04046
Dyes

Decart Inc.
Lamoille Industrial Park
Box 208
Morrisville
Vermont 05661
Deka transfer paints and permanent fabric paints

Dharma Trading Co.
P.O. Box 916
San Rafael
CA 94902
Procion dyes, silk dyes, all tie-dye and batik materials

Farquhar International Ltd
56 Harvester Avenue
Batavia
NY 14020
Dylon dyes

Pentalic Corporation Inc.
122 West 22nd Street
New York
Rowney Screen and Fabric Printing colours

Savoir-Faire
3020 Bridgeway
Suite 305
Sausalito
CA 94965
Silk dyes and equipment

Winsor & Newton Inc.
122 555 Winsor Drive
Secausus
New Jersey 07094
Printex Fabric Printing colour

Yarns

Appleton Bros. of London
West Main Road
Little Compton
Rhode Island 02837

Paternayan Bros. Inc.
312 East 95th Street
New York 10028

BOOK LIST

Dyeing

KAFKA, Francis J., *Batik, Tie-dyeing, Stencilling, Silk Screen, Block Printing*, Dover Publications

MAILE, Anne, *Tie-and-Dye Made Easy*, Mills and Boon 1971

ROBINSON, Stuart and Patricia, *Beginners' Guide to Fabric Dyeing and Printing*, Newnes 1982

SAMUEL, Evelyn, *Batik*, Batsford 1977

Embroidery

AVERY, Virginia. *Quilts to Wear*, Bell & Hyman 1980

BUTLER, Anne, *Batsford Encyclopaedia of Embroidery Stitches*, Batsford 1979

CLUCAS, Joy, *Your Machine for Embroidery*, Bell 1973

HOWARD, Constance, *The Constance Howard Book of Stitches*, Batsford 1979

SHORT, Eirian, *Quilting: Technique, Design and Application*, Batsford 1974

TIMMINS, Alice, *Patchwork: Technique and Design*, Batsford 1980

INDEX

Numbers *in italic* refer to numbers of illustrations

Appliqué *see* Embroidery techniques
Approaches 14–17, 18, 43, 57, 67, 75, 79, 81, 98, 108
Background fabrics:
  batik *colour plate 3*, 70–2
  sprayed and painted *colour plates 6 & 7*, 99
  tie-dyed *colour plates 2 & 4, 4, 23, 42*, 43, 50, 53
  tritik *43*, 54
Batik 57–80
  'crackle' *46, 53, 59, 63, 65*, 97
  dyes 21–2
  embroidery on *colour plate 3, 46, 51a, 54, 55, 58, 59, 60, 64, 65*, 79–80
  equipment 47, 57–61
  experiments 67–80
  fabrics 61
  method *50, 62*, 63–7, 75
  preparation of fabric 63
  removal of wax 67
  tjaps *47, 49, 60, 61, 66, 72*
  transferring design 63
  waxing 63, 68–72
Beading *see* Embroidery techniques
Discharge dyeing *29, 42*
Drawing:
  equipment 97
  experiments *81, 89*, 99
Dyes and dyeing:
  batik 14–22, *50, 62*, 75–9
  colour experiments 18, 43, 44, 50, 53

discharge *29, 42*
ombré and part dyeing 56
penetration of 18, 25
threads *30, 42*

Effects:
  birds *67*
  brushed *51, 55, 57, 64*, 70–2
  chevrons *10, 11*, 26–7, *33*
  'crackle' *46, 52, 53, 59, 63, 65, 67*
  dots *27b*, 38, *48*, 68
  feather 46
  fern 46
  fish *33*, 46
  geometric *32, 44, 81, 93, 98, 108*
  landscapes 59, *64, 84, 86, 87, 102*
  lines *27a*, 38, *48*, 54, 70
  mottled *22, 23*, 35, 53
  plant *40, 41, 42*, 50, *62, 66, 68, 69, 70, 72, 75, 75, 96*
  random batik *colour plate 2*, 67
  random tritik *43*, 54
  realistic *52*, 55, *59, 63*, 68
  sky *4*, 43, 67
  sprayed *66b*, 67, *83, 91, 92, 99, 103*
  stamped batik 68
  stencilled *70*, 75, *77*, 90–2
  sunburst *38, 39*, 50
  tree 35, *37*, 50, *59, 72*
  underwater *33, 44*, 46
  vegetation 44, *66*
  water *57a, 70*, 115

Embroidery techniques:
  appliqué *colour plate 3*, 15, 54, *66b*, *67b*,
    90, *95*, *102*, *103*, *104*, 116–19
  beading *79*, 80, *82*, *105*, *106*, 119–21
  canvaswork *colour plates 1 & 5*, 15, *17*, 99
  colour 14, 16
  highlights 14, 116
  machine embroidery *colour plate 7*, 58,
    66b, *84*, *88*, *89*, 97, *112*
  manipulating fabrics *109*, 123–5
  patchwork 15, *57b*, 71, *107*, *108*, 121–3
  quilting 14, *33*, *36*, 46, *96*, *98*, *99*, *100*, *101*,
    107, 113–16
  stitchery *1*, *2*, *5*, *18*, *24*, *32*, *33*, *45*, *59*, 80,
    92, 108–12
  texture 14, 27, 50, 79, 110, 113, 115, 119,
    125
Equipment:
  batik *47*, 57–61
  drawing 97–8
  painting and spraying 81
  stencilling 81
  tie-dye 18–21
Experiments:
  batik 67–80
  painting and spraying 98–104
  tie-dye 18, 25–35, 43–53
  tritik 35–41, 54–6

Fabrics:
  for batik 14, 61
  fibre content appendix I
  for drawing 97
  manmade and synthetic fibres 21, appen-
    dix I
  natural fibres 21, appendix I
  for spraying and painting 14, 84
  suitability for painting and dyeing
    appendix II
  for tie-dye 14, 21, 35
  for transfer printing 95
  transparent, use of 15, 44, 50, 56, 119
Fixing colour:
  fabric paints 84, 87
  silk paints *78*, 95
  transfer paints and crayons 95

Garments *48*, 84, *90*, 110, 115, 116, 119, 125
  jackets 46, 114

motif *89*
trimmings 53, 119
waistcoats *36*, 46, 56, *96*, *109*, 114

Household articles *94*, *98*, *99*, 102–4
  curtains 54
  cushions 46, 55, *75*, 79, *100*, 115, *107*
  quilts 54, 79, 114, 123

Machine embroidery *see* Embroidery techniques
Manipulating fabrics *see* Embroidery techniques
Methods:
  batik 63–7
  drawing 97
  ombré and part dyeing *28*, 41–2
  painting 86–8, 90
  pastel dye sticks 97
  silk paints 93
  spattering *73*, 90
  spraying *70*, *71*, 88–92
  stencilling *74*, *76*, 90
  tie-dye 25–35
  transfer paints and crayons *80*, 95
  tritik *25*, *27*, 35–41

Ombré and part dyeing *28*, 41–2

Painting and spraying 81–107
  embroidery *colour plates 6 & 7*, *66b*, *67b*,
    68, *72*, *75*, *77*, *79*, *82*, *83*, *84*, *86*, *87*, *88*, *92*
  equipment 81
  experiments 98–107
  fabrics 84
  methods 86–92
  paints 84
  transferring designs 63
Patchwork *see* Embroidery techniques
Prints *67*, *69*, 87, *93*, *94*, 107

Quilting *see* Embroidery techniques

Rubbings 97, 107

Silk paints 92–4
Spraying *70*, *71*, *72*, *73*, 88–92
Stencils *70*, *74*, *75*, *76*, *77*, *83*, 88, *86*, 90–2,
  92, *96*, *98*, 98–104
Stitches *see* Embroidery techniques

Tie-dye   18–56
    binding   *15*, 28, *38*, *39*, 44
    clamping   *13*, *14*, 28, *32*, 44
    discharge dyeing   *29*, 42
    dowels, sticks, hardboard shapes   *16*, *17*,
      18, *19*, *35*, *36*, *37*, 46–50
    dyes   21–4
    embroidery   *colour plates 2 & 4*, *18*, *24*, *32*,
      33, *36*, *45*
    equipment   18–21
    experiments   43–53
    folding   *8*, *9*, *10*, *11*, *12*, *13*, 25–8, 44
    marbling   *4*, *6*, *7*, 25, *35*, 43–4
    methods   25–43
    ombré and part dyeing   *28*, 41, 56
    rolling over a cord   *22*, *23*, 35, 53
    tritik   *24*, *25*, *26*, *27*, 35–41, *43*, *44*, *45*, 54–6
    using objects   *20*, *21*, 33, *38*, *39*, 50

Tone, alteration of   11, 110
Transfer paints and crayons   *front cover*, *79*,
    80, 95–7, 104–107
Transferring designs:
    batik   63
    painting and spraying   63
    transfer printing   *80*, 95
Tritik   35–41, 54–6
    dots   *27*, 38
    embroidery   *frontispiece*, *24*, *26*, *45*
    experiments   54–6
    gathering   *25*, *26*, 35
    outlines   *24*, 27, 38, *45*
    oversewing   *25*, 38
    tucks   *25*, *26*, 38

Window mount   *3*, 17, 46